MOVING BEYOND
HEALING THE TRAUMA OF PHYSICAL
AND SEXUAL ABUSE
THROUGH THETAHEALING®

JUDY DRAGON
THETAHEALING® MASTER, CHT, MINISTER

ROLLING THUNDER PUBLISHING
1615 Curlew Drive
Ammon, Idaho 83406

Rolling Thunder Publishing
Ammon, Idaho 83406

This Workbook is Dedicated to My Mother, Miriam Krostar Dragon

*I'm so glad that I can still talk to you though your body is gone.
In all that happened, you taught me the deepest level
of forgiveness possible. I knew that as I completely forgave you,
forgiveness would be more than possible with others.
And this has changed my life in the most profound ways.
I love you in ways that were impossible when you were alive.
Thank you for birthing me so I could be alive and present now!*

Table of Contents

FOREWARD   vi

INTRODUCTION   1

   Beliefs to clear/Teachings for ThetaHealing®

   practitioners   5

TYPES OF PHYSICAL AND SEXUAL ABUSE   7

UNDERSTANDING ABUSE FROM A BRAIN AND

   PHYSIOLOGICAL LEVEL   9

SIGNS OF CHILDHOOD ABUSE IN ADULTS   11

Witnessing trauma can be traumatic   12

MEMORIES   15-25

   Recalling memories   15

   Repression of "unwanted" memories   16

   Pattern of unveiling   18

   Spontaneous memories   18

   Image memories   19

   Dreams that are memories   19

   Body or somatic memories   20

   Acting-out memories   21

   Repressed feeling memories   22

   Accordion memories   22

   Grisly or bizarre memories   23

   Implanted memories   23

   Screen memories   25

HEALING OF CONSCIOUS AND

REPRESSED MEMORIES   27-75

   Ways to allow repressed memories to surface naturally   27

Fear of reliving the abuse   29

   Fear of feeling   29

   Beliefs to test/dig/clear/Creator's teachings   30-31

Fear of being in the body   32

Beliefs to test/dig/clear/Creator's teachings	33-35
Fear of or anger towards God/Creator	35-39
Beliefs to test/dig/clear/ Creator's teachings	37-39
THE UNDERSTANDING OF BOUNDARIES	40-46
Beliefs to test/dig/clear/Creator's teachings	43-46
BETRAYAL OF TRUST	46-50
Beliefs to test/dig/clear/Creator's teachings	47-50
BONDING AS ABUSE	50-52
FETAL ABUSE HEALING	52-53
INNER CHILD/REN HEALING	53-57
Meet your Inner Child Meditation	55-59
THE CONTINUUM OF DISSOCIATION	59-61
APPROACHING A CLIENT ABOUT	
WHAT YOU "SEE" INTUITIVELY	62-66
Beliefs to test/dig/clear/Creator's teachings	65-66
MEMORY RETRIEVAL–HOW TO PROCEED	67-69
The Rescue	70-73
Verifying Emerging or Recovered Memories	73-76
Patterns of Awareness	75-76
CLEARING ANCESTRAL LINEAGE THAT HOLDS	
ABUSE PATTERNING/Creator's teachings	77-79
HEART SONG EXERCISE	80
FORGIVENESS	81-85
MOVING BEYOND ABUSE	86-87
EPILOGUE	88-89
Creator's teachings	89
RESPONSIBILITY TO REPORT CHILD ABUSE	
BY A MINISTER	90-91
FOOTNOTES REFERENCES	92-96
RECOMMENDED BOOKS	97-98
GLOSSARY	99-103
INDEX	104-108

Foreward

This workbook is a compilation of almost twenty-five years of working professionally with people who have been physically and sexually abused as children. They have taught me about the courage and the resiliency of the human body and spirit through the darkest of the dark. Our souls learn and/or bring forth healing to ourselves and to others in some dramatic ways. Healing from trauma is not only completely possible, but a true reality through Creator-of-All. You might not find this statement in conventional psychological textbooks, but I know it to be true. It is my own personal experience and in witnessing with others.

For several years now, friends in the ThetaHealing® community have asked me to write down how I work with my clients who have been abused. I kept saying that it's too much to empty my brain with all that I've experienced in this field. I didn't have time because I was writing two other books, teaching workshops, working privately with clients, and dancing on a salsa team. I wanted to make sure there was a time to sleep.

After teaching an Advance workshop in June '09, as so much abuse memories had surfaced for the participants, I decided to give the class some quick ways to be present and work with other students. When the class was over, those who were interested could stay and take notes. It was only a half of a page.

Afterwards, I decided to type what I had jotted down and out came this flowing stream of information. For most part of July, I stayed up to 3 AM writing to my heart's content. It was so peaceful and relaxing to just let this information and inspiration finally take form. My shoulders didn't even get tight from being at the computer for hours. I just felt so blessed that my fingers can type fast and that I have a Capricornian organizational mind because the end result truly surprised me. Writing, for me, is like digging on beliefs... you don't know where it's all going to go, but you somehow trust you're guided, and there is a completion that will make a shift in consciousness whether it be mine or someone else's.

I want to thank Creator-of-All for the inspiration and healing IT continues to make available to me. To Vianna for giving me a most precious gift, in taking me "up" to remember my connection to Creator-of-All and teaching me ThetaHealing®. To Sidnee Cox, Eric Brumett, Beth Rachel, and Jane Pritchard for their loving support and listening ears. And to all my clients whose courage and amazing strength to heal continue to inspire me--my deepest gratitude for sharing the depth of your lives with me.

Introduction

This workbook is geared toward assisting ThetaHealing® practitioners to work with clients who have trauma due to sexual and/or physical abuse using educational and practical techniques connected to Creator-of-All.

I realize that psychological and emotional abuse can create enormous devastation. I feel that the regular ThetaHealing® courses give plenty of support in working with emotional trauma. I have grouped psychological abuse under physical abuse, though I won't be covering it specifically. There will also be several other kinds of abuse mentioned later, though they too will not be covered at this time.

Due to the vastness of the field of abuse, I will only briefly go over the types of physical and sexual abuse, physiological issues, signs of abuse, types of memories, how memories are repressed, False Memory Foundation, techniques in healing that can be Creator directed, forgiveness, moving beyond, and your responsibility as a minister/ ThetaHealer® in reporting abuse. My purpose is really to give some easy guidelines to help you be the best facilitator possible when digging and trauma presents itself, is discovered, or you feel the client is ready to deal with the abuse that you "see" intuitively.

In being part of the Theta community since 1998, I have not only seen but have had others tell me of their experiences with teachers, practitioners, and students who were unable to help them when deep sexual or physical abuse issues surfaced during a session or class. I have also personally experienced other practitioners being unable to hold a safe and supportive "container" to process memories or find the beliefs below the memories. Clients have been abandoned mid-session in tears, told that what they were experiencing wasn't true or a past life (when it was from their childhood) or left dissociated and ungrounded. I am not sharing this to make others wrong. We, as ThetaHealers®, need to be educated and emotionally prepared for whatever issues surface during a session. We are responsible for clearing our own issues so we can stay fully present for others.

Theta teachers have reported their fears of working with students or clients who have deep-seated trauma. "What do I do?" "Where do I go with this?" As with any part of ThetaHealing®, whether it be "seeing" a disease you've never witnessed before or identifying an organ psychically, having a context for what you have witnessed through Creator-of-All can make all the difference.

It is my sincerest desire to empower the ThetaHealing® community in being fully present to release fears in working with clients (or yourself) with childhood abuse issues, and to help the community be informed so we can step into sessions with supportive skills and confidence.

I realize that many practitioners want to limit the type of clientele that they work with, but considering that 1 in 3 women and 1 in 5 men have been sexually abused under the age of 18[1], and there are 1.7 million reports of child abuse each year [the number of reported cases is small compared with the number of actual cases][2], your chances of no one coming in with these issues are slim.

For teachers, look around your classroom and realize that quite a few people have been abused and may not know it. Do you realize that over 95% of people in Alcoholics Anonymous, Overeaters Anonymous or Debtors Anonymous (those with addictions) have been abused?[3] Sexual and physical abuse affects every area of our lives whether it happened to us or to another. You can see that the world has a great deal of healing to clear and each one of us can help be part of that transformation in the highest and best way if we choose.

Trauma and abuse can start not only in the womb but in memories from other lifetimes that are stored in the body. I'm sure many of you have experienced the healing of "past life" memories that got stuck in the body and in the consciousness. But trauma that is repressed in this lifetime gets confused with being a past life experience quite often. Vianna has said that people find it easier to go to a past life than wanting to deal with what happened in this lifetime.

My focus, though, is to share techniques that will help those who have either conscious or repressed trauma from this lifetime to release memories and feelings to the surface, and clear completely. This entails helping the client feel safe enough to deal with the trauma whether cognizant of it or not.

I realize that there are many schools of thought about this process. There are researchers, therapists and Theta practitioners who feel that memories of past incidences of abuse are insignificant in helping a person be present and should just be by-passed. This is similar to what one may often hear in a dysfunction family, "Get on with your life!" I beg to differ in saying that avoidance is not a good way to heal. Practitioners as well as clients are afraid to go deep. I have heard Theta Teachers say "You are just stuck in mind candy." This statement is not going to give a safe place for revealing the client's history and release the memories and beliefs. Would a practitioner say this to a person who is dying from cancer? Trauma and abuse is indeed part of the earthly paradigm in time and space. Vianna has repeatedly shared that if a client doesn't want to look at the past and only at the present, there are issues in the past.

Some feel that remembering past traumatic incidences will put the person in trauma again. This could happen if not properly facilitated. For the practitioners who witness another's traumatic memories, it is also possible for them to experience secondary Post Traumatic Syndrome[4] if they are ungrounded in being a witness to the client's history. Your strong connection to Creator-of-All and clearing your own issues will make you a superb facilitator.

There are groups of scientists and researchers who feel traumatic memories should be eliminated chemically. In fact, there are pills and brainwashing techniques to do just this.[5] [6] I'm in deep gratitude for those who have spoken against such means because it is already being misused covertly. If you have ever seen the movie 'Eternal Sunshine of a Spotless Mind", realize that this kind of technology does exist and is used for purposes of memory erasing and mind control.[7]

There are a few who feel that every traumatic memory we've ever had has to be processed. This perception will keep a client having a life of stress with little hope for creating something better. Again, I say that it depends on how this process of remembering and healing is facilitated that will affect the client in the highest and best way. I am a proponent of remembering what the Spirit/Soul feels it's to release. I feel that there is a timing of one's process and the information will release to remember in its proper timing and sequence. Healing from deep seated trauma is a God Process meaning that one's willingness with Creator leads the way.

The Ego, though, can easily sabotage or block the remembering to continue the illusion of a false reality which appears to feel safe. Vianna once said that forgetting takes more energy than to remember. Can you imagine what happens to the body in repressing trauma? Can you imagine a pressure cooker of energy? Are you aware that many of the immune suppression diseases can be linked to childhood abuse?[8]

Truth is not difficult to remember, or witness in healing if we stay connected to Creator-of-All. It's denial, projection and internalization (self blame) that creates havoc.

Beliefs to Clear

Beliefs to test/dig/clear for ThetaHealing® teachers and practitioners that might have fears of working with clients who were physically or sexually abused.

- ◇ I fear working with physical abuse issues in others.
- ◇ I fear guiding clients to physical abuse memories that are unknown.
- ◇ I fear working with sexual abuse issues in others .
- ◇ I fear guiding clients to sexual abuse memories that are unknown.
- ◇ I fear working on issues that may be buried within myself around sexual abuse...physical abuse.
- ◇ It's easier to forget than to remember.
- ◇ I will be hurt if I work with clients who have been abused.
- ◇ Clients who have been abused are damaged (we are to see their wholeness).
- ◇ The effects of physical abuse are impossible to completely heal.
- ◇ The effects of sexual abuse are impossible to completely heal.
- ◇ Physical abuse *has to* take a long time to heal.
- ◇ Physical abuse takes a long time to heal.
- ◇ Sexual abuse *has to* take a long time to heal.
- ◇ Sexual abuse takes a long time to heal.
- ◇ It's my client's fault that they were abused.
- ◇ Physical abuse cleanses humanity (males, females) of their sins.
- ◇ Sexual abuse cleanses humanity (males, females) of their sins.
- ◇ Creator is absent (for others...for me) when abuse occurs.
- ◇ Creator abandons others...me... when trauma/abuse occurs.

Teachings for ThetaHealing®
Teachers and Practitioners
(through Creator's perspective,
understanding and/or definition)
[in all cases, w/ means "with" and w/o means "without"]

◇ I know what it feels like and how to be safe in working with people who have been physically abused...sexually abused.

◇ I know when I am safe to work with people who have been physical abused...sexually abused.

◇ I know what it feels like, how to, and when to hold a safe space for others to reveal physical abuse memories... sexual abuse memories.

◇ I know what it feels like and how to be safe when others reveal physical abuse memories...sexual abuse memories.

◇ I know how to listen to one who has been physically abused...sexually abused... w/o feeling traumatized.

◇ I know what it feels like and how to feel confident in being present while staying connected to Creator with clients who have been physically abused...sexually abused.

◇ I know what it feels like and how to live w/o secondary PTSD.

◇ I know what it feels like and how to be emotionally prepared to work with physically abused clients...w/ sexually abused clients.

◇ I know how to work with people who have been physically or sexually abused w/o anxiety...w/o fear.

◇ I understand that Creator-of-All orchestrates and is present for every session I do with a client.

Types of Physical and Sexual Abuse

As I mentioned in the introduction, abuse covers an enormous field. For general information, I have categorized the acts of abuse, both physically and sexually, below. You are welcome to add more. Many of the actions are found in both categories particularly in ritual, government, and alien abuse. These realities do exist on this 3rd Plane of Existence and have been mentioned by Vianna during lectures as well. I have worked with clients who have experienced such abuse and trauma. As ThetaHealers®, we cannot be blind to Creator's Truth. And you certainly have a choice to work with these kinds of clients or not. Education and applicable tools assist you to expand your paradigms as Creator's practitioners.

I consider neglect under physical abuse though it is often categorized by itself...that would seem par-for-the-course in being left alone.[9]

Remember that abuse/trauma can occur anywhere, from the home to battlefields.

Physical Abuse:

- Being hit, spanked, punched, beat, battered
- Hung by feet or arms/hands
- Stepped on or kicked
- Pulled by hair
- Tickled excessively

- Shaken, thrown, choked
- Cut, bitten
- Burned
- Neglect
- Starvation
- Torture variations- Water submersion, electro-shock, put in ice or scalding water, sleep deprivation, psychic driving (page 103), body mutilation, etc.
- Psychological (kidnapping, war, terrorism, hostage, ritual and government mind control/brainwashing)
- Government experimentation (such as injection of diseases and toxins, Manchurian candidates/assassination mind control programming, manipulations of DNA, cloning, remote viewing, spying, virtual reality, and teleportation)
- Alien Experimentation—(exploratory, non-medical implantation, rape, egg harvesting, hybriding, DNA changes)

Sexual Abuse:

- Verbal sexual innuendos and harrassment
- Inappropriate touching: fondling, licking of genitals, mouth, ears, breasts of children
- Genital exposure; forced masturbation
- Digital (hand/finger) penetration
- Oral, genital, or anal rape
- Vaginal/genital mutilation and circumcision
- Making children read pornographic material or performing in pornographic movies/snuff films
- Involvement in prostitution/child sex slavery
- Forced bestiality
- Ritual abuse (including Satanism and Black Witchcraft—invocation of demonic entities, rape, torture, mutilation, sexual slavery, murder, sacrifice, and mind control programming)

Understanding Abuse from a Brain & Physiological Level

Childhood abuse can have lasting effects on the entire brain and body if not healed. High-stress early environments for children create problems in attention regulation and self-control which often causes hyperactivity, anxiety, and/or difficulties with inhibiting destructive impulses.

The interaction between our environment and the DNA plays a crucial role in determining our resistance to stress thus the risk for suicide. The function of the DNA is not fixed like once theorized. Epigenetic marks, the study of how a person's genes are constantly remodeled in response to life experiences (the more positive experiences you have, the stronger your genes will become) are the product of this interaction.[10]

A research study from Douglas Mental Health University Institute found a gene, NR3CI, which influences the brain's susceptibility to stress hormones. It was less likely to be activated in people who have been abused. Those who have been abused had lower levels of expression in the gene for the glucocorticoid (cortisol) receptor, which is critical for the stress response pathway. This kind of gene expression, in adaptation to trauma especially early in life, becomes a "state of mind, brain, and body" around which subsequent experiences organize.[11] On a spiritual level, this is an exemplary explanation of how we arrange our realities from our experiences. This is not to blame those who have been abused but allow the practitioner the understanding of the spiritual perceptions in reality patterning.

Children who are abused early are flooded with stress hormones like adrenaline and cortisol, impacting on how the brain develops and affects the stress regulation system. In being flooded with fight-or-flight hormones, fear is maintained and can become pathological.[12] This in turn puts impact on the hippocampus, the area which controls feelings, meaning that adults abused as children will be more likely to be highly stressed, have difficulties with anger and emotions, and be prone to self-harm, anxiety, suicide and depression.[13] Have you ever considered that such disorders as some cases of OCD, Bi-polar, Schizophrenia, Borderline schizophrenia, and all Dissociative Disorders might originate from abuse?[14] [15]

There is a decrease of cortex activity and an increase of limbic system sensitivity (responsible for emotions), decreased hippocampal volume (memory function is impaired...related to psychiatric disorders like PTSD and depression), impact on the left and right hemisphere, underdevelopment of left brain (control of language), a smaller corpus callosum (less integration of the hemispheres which can lead to dramatic shifts in mood or personality), and neuro-endocrine alterations (affects a range of basic psychological and physiological functions).[16]

Research shows adults with histories of child abuse can respond to minor triggers with a range of catastrophic reactions. This is because these people become increasingly responsive to relatively minor stimuli as a result of decreased frontal lobe functioning (learning and problem solving) and increased limbic system (amygdala) sensitivity (impulsiveness).[17]

Yale Child Study Center found that the brain areas in abused children have fewer synapses or neural connections.[18] There can also be a decreased production of thyroid hormone which regulates metabolism.

Signs of Childhood Abuse in Adults

Outward signs of adults with symptoms of childhood abuse can vary. Some adults become overachievers and appear extremely successful in the world. Others end up on the street, homeless or in mental or penal institutions. People cope the best way they can given their connection to their inner strength and their soul journey. All through this stream of awareness, choices are given to each of us in how to change life patterns to help evolve in more fulfilling ways. As practitioners, we are not here to judge the conditions or journey in any way.

Your connection with Creator-of-All and scanning the body will reveal a great deal (look at the patterning in the colon and brain around abuse). Listening to the client describe their life and their relationship with their family leads to ways in identifying possible patterns of abuse. One symptom does not mean a person was abused physically or sexually. Check in with Creator.

Compared with people without a history of childhood abuse, adults with such a history are more likely to have: no or little memories of childhood, "spliced memories" of childhood (i.e. remembering going to a store and leaving but not remembering what happened while there), out-of-body experience to escape; substance abuse or a partner with a substance abuse problem; anxiety disorders; depression; OCD; suicidal ideation or behavior; unintended pregnancy; self-injury; abuse their own children or refuse to properly discipline their children; dissociative disorders; schizophrenia; aberrant behaviors;

eating disorders; sleep disorders; sexual dysfunction or promiscuity; lack of pain sensation; chronic head, face or pelvic pain; musculo-skeletal complaints; gastrointestinal distress or symptoms; asthma or other respiratory ailments; weight and self-image issues; pseudo-neurologic symptoms (dizziness, etc.). [19]

Keep in mind that if clients come in with scarcity or financial issues, abundance flows best when the first and second chakras are open. This means that if a person has been physically or sexually abused or the body or energy registers that way in those chakras, negative programs will need to be cleared so the abundance can once again come into balance.

Lori Kondora, a nurse who interviewed adult women who had been sexually abused as children, found that while many women experienced low self-esteem, depression, addictive behaviors, anxiety, pain and eating disorders, some women also experienced resilience, independence, creativity, a deeper spirituality, and personal strength. **Remembering was central to the beginning of the healing process and telling their stories to others enhanced that process.**[20]

Witnessing Trauma can be Traumatic

A client can witness trauma when he or she was young. There are different effects in how the child unconsciously copes with such situations. This is why it is so important to keep children away from violent TV, movies and video games. The process of desensitization can start early, and the child can have difficulty growing up connected to their feelings.

Coping strategies:

1. They might take the situation on energetically as if it happened to them. There is a dissociation or confusion in who it was happening to physically.

Check:

- ◇ I know how to tell the difference between what happened and the energy I took on from the occurrence.
- ◇ I know the difference between what happened in my childhood and who it happened to.

2. In believing that they have to protect another, though it may not have been physically threatening to them, they hold the energy of the attack within themselves. They might hold onto a soul fragment or give a soul fragment to the other person being hurt (page 175-176 of Basic Theta textbook). They might share their life force with another. **You can command to return not only soul fragments but the separate life forces. It's very powerful!**

Life Force Separated and Returned

Command to witness the life force around and connected to the client as it separates in what was intermingled with another. The original life force returns to the client.

Check:

- ◇ I have to give up a part of myself to save my family...
  a sibling...a parent...another child...a friend...a pet.

3. They could internalize by blaming themselves for not being able to do something to stop the abuse. In-other-words, they unconsciously think that their suffering, guilt or strength will help the person being abused. You will find that this often happens in both physically violent homes and in witnessing sexual abuse of other siblings or friends. This must be ascertained by your connection to Creator so you can guide the person.

Check:

- ◇ It's my fault for being unable to stop the abuse.
- ◇ I blame myself for others actions.
- ◇ I have to use my suffering...my guilt...my strength to save another.

4. Emotional incest, taking care of the emotional needs of an adult, can lead empathic children to interpret intentions of an adult whose energy feels malevolent, violent or sexual, as having been abused.

Work on issues around boundaries and separating the needs, thoughts, feelings, ideas and opinions of others from the client's needs, thoughts, feelings, ideas, and opinions. Teach the client how to be a priority in their own life w/o feeling guilty or selfish. Teach them what it feels like for their needs to matter and count. Make sure to check any oaths, vows, promises, trades and contracts that might stop them from being a priority person in their life.

Memories

> "Your mind is in every cell of your body."
> – *David Felten Ph.D.; University of Rochester School of Medicine*

Recalling Memories

How our minds protect us from harm is quite amazing. It functions to keep anything that we have found unacceptable or unpleasant in an unconscious form as an attempt to protect us from anxiety, panic, and trauma. However, these repressive defenses can get "leaky" as the mind builds and stores up so many experiences, and eventually, they break into our consciousness in some form.

Over a century ago, Freud proposed that unwanted memories can be excluded from awareness through a process called *repression*. It is unknown, however, how repression occurs in the brain. The repression process is a completely automatic psychological defense against trauma and does not involve conscious intent. In contrast, deliberately pushing something out of awareness because you want to avoid any responsibility for it is called *suppression*.[21]

Through studying different parts of the brain, researchers were able to confirm the existence of an active forgetting process and establish a neurobiological model for guiding inquiry into motivated forgetting.[22]

More recently, it was established that the frontal cortex is involved in recalled (conscious) memories. Current thinking holds that new memories are encoded in the hippocampus and then eventually transferred to the frontal lobes for long-term storage.[23] Conscious, recalled memories are mostly in the frontal brain and have dimensional quality.

Many clients have always remembered their abuse, and may even recognize some of the patterns that are created from the abuse but have dissociated feelings around it. They expect that the actual perceptions of the "feeling," if connected to the event, will overwhelm them, possibly plunging them into despair and depression or catastrophic action. However, the mind is always trying to make "connections," and while it is possible to sometimes have these connections appear to stay dormant, it usually costs the person a great deal of mental energy to keep this data repressed.[24]

There are many ways to enhance remembering. According to researchers from Manchester Metropolitan University in England, moving your eyes horizontally, from side-to-side for about 30 seconds, may be all it takes to give your memory a boost. The researchers suspect it's because the horizontal eye movements cause the two hemispheres of the brain to interact more, and communication between the left and right brain hemispheres is known to help us remember certain things.[25]

Repression of "Unwanted " Memories

The kinds of memories which are not from conscious awareness, repressed memories, are processed in different parts of the brain—the amagdyla and hippocampus, which are part of the limbic system--and are dreamlike, hazy and dissociative in quality. Like intuitively "seeing," many of the senses-- hearing, smell, sight, taste, feeling--bring forth the fluid perceptions of the subconscious mind.

A person won't bring repressed memories to the conscious mind by just sitting there, in a cognizant state, while trying to remember. If memories are to surface, they are pieced together through clues from past patterning, dreams, images, and the body. Intuitively, the practitioner may witness a cloud of energy around the client or compartmentalization in the brain which signifies amnesic barriers. The memories are within this energy and the beliefs lie beneath or within it. Using energy testing with the fingers helps to see if the person believes an event is true both at a conscious and unconscious level.

There is an incredible synchronicity of events that will guide the client to remember. Repressed memories often surface when some event occurs to "awaken" the person. It could be when a client's biological child becomes a certain age that triggers the client's remembering of s/he being at that age when abused. It could be the death of a family member who had hurt the adult as a child. There could be a car accident that jolts a part of the mind to start remembering. It could be bottoming out from drug use, a near death experience, money issues or lower back problems. The soul supports the psyche to remember so it can heal.

If you "see" or suspect repressed memories, check with Creator if it's good timing to bring it up. Some people have been working on their issues or beliefs only to keep looping to the same ones over and over without being able to clear them. I have witnessed that these kinds of clients will either be able to visualize the scene differently at one point, but then the same beliefs or resentments will occur again with the same depth of feelings; or the resentment or issue will not clear when visualized, and the client continues to get more and more frustrated. When I find this to occur, I look for dissociation or hidden trauma (sexual, ritual, Government, alien abuse).

Pattern of Unveiling

There can also be a pattern of unveiling of memories or past traumatic history. Once some of the patterns of general emotional or physical abuse are processed, sexual abuse can surface because the person feels safe enough to deal with it. I've heard from many clients, "I've worked on my issues for years and now this shows up?" I tell them that all the work they've done up to this point has given them the strength and awareness to deal with this next level. Creator will sometimes not even fully reveal to the practitioner the levels of abuse in the client. Remember that on this Plane of Existence, timing tends to be important.

As sexual abuse is processed, ritual abuse, alien abductions or Government mind control could be revealed as well. The alien abduction may already be known due to implants the practitioner might find in the body. It's like the "peeling of the onion skin." This unveiling does NOT happen all the time. It's just something to keep in your awareness. You must check in with Creator.

*Spontaneous Memories (*Recall Memories)*

The essential factor in memories surfacing is the client's readiness to deal with the reality of the abuse. Sometimes the client will spontaneously remember due to a trigger or catalyst which sets the memory process in action. These kinds of memories are usually denied and not repressed. The client may have known about the abuse at some level, but avoided thinking about it. The memories are quite believable because of the coherent and consistent details.

Helen had a spontaneous memory when a 10 year old girl had been dropped off in front of her house on a main road by a stranger. It was 10 o'clock at night. The girl knocked on her door looking scared and confused. She said she had just been raped by a man who picked her up a few miles from where Helen had lived as a child. She was able to get in touch with the child's parents but after the episode, she remembered that she had been molested at 10 and hid it from everyone.

When beliefs or programs are discussed and/or changed, the client can start to see the patterns within the context of occurrences to identify abuse. Then images can come forth as the person puts the dots together.[26]

Image Memories

Images, blips, glimpses or flashbacks can spontaneously come from the unconscious when the timing is right for the client. The client will suddenly get a quick picture of something unrelated to what they were thinking or doing. The process can start with abuse incidents that flit through the client's mind at odd moments, *like a flash of a naked man standing over a child in bed or a belt in the cellar.*

There could also be innocent yet persistent images from childhood that arise out of nowhere that are the stored memory of the beginning or end of an abusive incident.

Donna saw a repeated image of herself as a 5 year old in her bathing suit going to the neighbor's pool. She didn't think much about it until it turned out that that was where she was lured to be sexually abused.

Dreams that are Memories

Repressed memories can also come as nightmares, repeated anxiety dreams or acting-out memories. *One of my clients would dream of four snakes that terrorized her. She would wake herself up with her legs moving to escape. She ended up remembering four men in her family who had abused her and her attempts to get away.*

Body or Somatic Memories

> "The body never lies." *–Martha Graham*

Our bodies react to everything that happens to us. The more traumatic the occurrence, the more impact there is on the body. Body memories are sensations that symbolically or literally capture some aspect of the trauma. Sensory impulses are recorded in the parietal lobes of the brain, and these remembrances of bodily sensations can be felt when similar occurrences or cues (triggers) re-stimulate the stored memories.[27] When the "trauma energy" from abuse cannot be "released", it is then "converted into symptoms."[28]

One of the notable symptoms of abuse is distortion or loss of the olfactory sense due to head trauma and oral penetration. Smells trigger memories.

I have had clients who, in discussing what happened to them, would get immediately nauseas, light-headed and their groin would hurt. I have worked with men who were abused, and their testicles or anus would become painful when they remembered their abuse. I had a client whose leg doubled in size overnight to where she could not even put her shoe on. When she remembered what had happened, her leg immediately went back to normal size within one hour.

A client may have been through the medical arena attempting to find out either what their symptoms are about or how to stop the persistence only to be told that there is nothing wrong with them. Somatic responses can cause symptoms that cannot be detected in lab tests or routine examinations by doctors. Other somatic memories that can arise without a defined medical reason can be: persistent headaches and migraines; stiff neck; intestinal tract problems (constipation, diarrhea, cramping); irregular menses; visual disturbances; tinnitus; palpitations (racing heart), sweating; chills (hot/cold flashes); TMJ issues (difficulties in opening the mouth, jaw clenching or spasming or teeth grinding); inability to be touched on certain parts of the body without fear or panic; numbness of certain body parts; inability to feel sexual pleasure; impotence or frigidity; painful intercourse; endometriosis; persistent muscle spasms; tremors; sleep disorders.

As the client heals in releasing the memories, and beliefs are changed to support the client and their body in being present for their needs, the body memories will relinquish their grip.

Acting-out Memories

When a forgotten/unconscious memory is spontaneously expressed or acted-out through some physical action, it is referred to as an "Acting-out memory." It involves a verbal or bodily act in response to something that reminds the client of the original episodes of trauma.[29]

I had a client who would pick the skin below her navel after sessions. We later discovered that there was a syringe that had been inserted in that area during an alien abduction to remove eggs. There was an actual physical small hole in that area.

Below is another common example of an acting-out memory. *One of my clients had been suspecting for awhile that she had been sexually abused, and the person was her uncle, her father's brother. During our conversation, in discussing the feelings she had around her uncle, she started to change the words to "my father." I asked her if she meant her uncle. This shocked her in hearing me repeat what she had said, and she realized soon after, that it was indeed her father who had abused her and not her uncle.* Call it a Freudian slip or a verbal acting-out memory—saying something that the person had no intention of saying—none-the-less, it is a form of remembering.

Repressed Feeling Memories

When we have memories of an event in our lives, such as a birth or death, there are often emotional reactions that arise. Basically, a feeling memory is an emotional response to a particular situation or event. If the person is triggered, whereas feelings from the unconscious surface, we can have feelings pertaining to the event without any conscious recall of the situation itself. Feeling memories are often experienced with a sense of "flooding" of unexplainable emotions particularly around abuse issues. A gut feeling or sense that something abusive happened as a child, is considered a feeling memory. You might hear the client say, *"I think I was sexually abused, but it's just a strange feeling."*

Years back, a man contacted me to set up an appointment for his teenage son who was acting out. I suggested I work with the man first. During the session, he mentioned that he thought he might have strangled his son several times when the boy was younger...he wasn't sure. I realized immediately why the boy might be acting out, and that not only did this man have a dissociative disorder but was having "feeling memories." (In realizing that I was dealing with a very unsafe and unstable person, I had Creator tell me exactly what to say in order to release him from any further sessions without triggering him. It worked out beautifully.)

Feeling memories are often accompanied with various other kinds of memories such as body memories. A stiff neck can bring on terror. Abdominal pain can create shame.

Accordion Memories

A memory may contain contradictory information which can be quite confusing for the client. Have you ever been a witness to a car accident with others? Each person perceives a different angle of the incident in relaying what has happened. The occurrence becomes a compilation. Consider the possibility that when a child is abused repeatedly in a similar manner, the memory can collapse two or more memories into one so that these separate elements of memories will create a composite. When memories occur as an adult, they expand like an accordion file exposing an entire set of related memories.

Grisly or Bizarre Memories

If a client's memories start to become unusually bizarre or grisly, with strange symbols or chanting sounds, it may be the beginning of ritual abuse memories. Ritual abuse is characterized by inhuman acts of physical, sexual and psychological tortures often involving groups of people performing atrocities in a pseudo-ceremonial or ceremonial settings.[30] It is most important to hold a space of possibility that these situations can occur, and they are not as rare as some would like to think.

Implanted Memories

Vianna has mentioned implanted memories in reference to therapists who somehow convince their clients that abuse happened to them even if it didn't. I agree that there are incompetent therapists in the field as there are in any healing profession; but more so, there has been a very powerful backlash that started in the late 1980's to stop adults abused as children from revealing and making public their abuse history. To stop those who had been victimized, the backlash has gone after the therapists. Many therapists have decided not to work with clients who have had deep abuse trauma because of the legal and physical harassment.

Implanted memories by therapists are much rarer than most think because trauma really needs to be implemented for such a memory to truly be implanted including shock, torture, and hypnosis with torture or drugs. Therapists tend to be a more cautious group at best, and the notion that they suddenly begin implanting false memories in tens of thousands of clients for no apparent reason strain credulity. Certainly no one has presented a shred of evidence for massive "false memory" implantation by therapists.[31]

This paranoia around therapists causing false memories has been propagated by the False Memory Syndrome Foundation which was started by professional psychologists, many perpetrators themselves and some connected to the CIA instigating a backlash. [32] One former False Memory Syndrome Foundation Advisory Board member told *Paidika: The Journal of Paedophilia* that, "Pedophiles can boldly and courageously affirm what they choose. They can say that what they want is to find the best way to love. With boldness they can say, 'I believe this is in fact part of God's will." [33]

Leading memory researchers, such as Dr. Bessel Van der Kolk of Harvard Medical School, maintain that traumatic memories, which typically are engraved in the sensorimotor processes, are not subject to the same kinds of contamination that can affect normal memory. Traumatic amnesia, described in the DSM-IV-TR as psychogenic amnesia, is a phenomenon which has been known to mental health professionals for more than 100 years. The clinically observed characteristics of traumatic memory formation and retrieval match precisely the patterns of memory recovery.

The positive side of this backlash against the disclosure of abuse is that therapists have had to clean up their therapeutic techniques and allow the client to reveal more thoroughly, even if they suspect abuse.

As intuitives, telling a person that something happened to them and then the client accepts it as their truth, could be considered an implanted thought form as well. People have free will to accept or reject thoughts. As practitioners, we always want to be tactful in what we say and how we word things especially to clients who seem emotionally fragile or vulnerable and trigger easily. And these kinds of clients also have a part in this relationship. Their discerning abilities are not very attuned so they accept another's truth or word without proper questioning or discretion. What we say can often be misconstrued or misinterpreted as well.

For clarity on what I consider real implanted memories, there are several covert technologies that create them. Besides hypnosis combined with drugs and torture, there is a form of virtual reality that makes the "victim" think that they were abused with scenes of incredible trauma. Virtual reality goggles are often placed on the child while being restrained. They might even be electrically shocked to anchor the reality of the implanted visuals. [34]

There are also implanted memories through an alien technology that places an implant receptor in copper around the cells to beam in memories in order to keep the person and their body traumatized. I have witnessed Creator changing such implants and the client immediately feeling better and different.

Screen Memories

Along similar lines, there exists screen memories which hide or screen another memory. For many years, screen memory meant a sensory memory fragment that carried the emotion of the entire event. Thus a child who was staring down at the floor while being hit might later only remember his or her shoes along with a vivid sense of shame and anger. This shows how the child has "spliced" the memory, editing out what was too difficult.

A screen memory could also be a partially true memory that an individual subconsciously creates because the actual memory is intolerable. For example, a client may report abuse by a distant cousin when actually the abuser was the client's brother. This disguised presentation allows the client time to adjust to aspects of the abuse before accepting the total reality of the situation.

For those who have been under mind control programming, a screen memory may be a real event or may be implanted by the programmer through hypnosis—staged scenes with appropriate costumes and props, movies, cartoons, or "virtual reality." Some people believe that memories of past lives, satanic ritual abuse, and alien abductions are examples of screen memories. The screen memory is designed to provoke disbelief and serves to protect a programming session or medical or psychological experiment. [35]

No matter whether a memory was implanted or not, it still needs to be cleared as the person's body and mind has taken on the trauma as if it was experienced at the time of the occurrence. The healing of mind control programming will not be covered in this text, but since this topic of implanted memories has been discussed by Vianna, I wanted to clarify and expound on it.

Healing of Conscious and Repressed Memories

> *"...And then the day came when the risk to remain tight in a bud was more painful than the risk it took to blossom."* —Anais Nin

When a conscious or repressed memory heals completely, there is no more emotional charge left. It's
like a plug that has been pulled from the wall outlet...electrical juice
stops running. It no longer controls the client's energetic/emotion-
al field or thought process. It can then be recalled as any conscious
memory might be that has no charge.

Ways to allow repressed memories to surface naturally for clients:

- The presence of the practitioner in being compassionate, patient,
  and non-judgmental supports the client to feel safe. Be clear in
  understanding the client's paradigm. Track them during the session.
- Work on the client's safety issues deeply.
- Take the client to the 7th Plane to experience the peace and safety
  of All-That-Is and have them go there everyday as a meditation,
  even several times per day.
- Guide the client to the 7th Plane so Creator will take them to the

memories if ready. I then use questions, similar to what is asked in guiding a client through a crystal layout or belief session, so the client can view what happened. Some may call this guided trance work or hypnosis, but Theta is the brainwave state that allows the practitioner to do this in whatever form it is called.

- Non-dominant handwriting allows the unconscious information to emerge. Have the client ask a question with the dominant hand and answer with non-dominant hand. The writing often looks like a young child's handwriting which is a good way to connect with the Inner Child. (see pages 53-57)

- Journal writing helps to record the memories as well as assisting the client to track and release the feelings and recognize the belief patterns. It can help the belief work go faster because of cognizant awareness.

- Drawing and art work support the very creative unconscious in releasing symbols or scenes. Have them look at the drawn characters' expressions or stance.

- Have the client put together a collage of childhood pictures in order of increasing age as s/he was growing up.

- Body/energy work supports the flow of energy to awaken the body's intelligence, to release stored-up cellular energy where the memories have been held, and stops the body from becoming too uncomfortable in releasing.

- Dance and movement allow the feelings to express from the body. Partner dancing also allows for a safe structure in order to be touched.

- Help the client create a support system which may include Theta-Healing® workshops and groups; therapy and therapy groups; online groups; 12 Step groups. The more resources, the better.

Fear of Reliving the Abuse

One of the biggest fears that come up for clients who are ready to deal with repressed memories is of reliving the abuse. There is a difference between reliving the abuse and remembering the past. Make sure your client knows the difference.

In abreaction, the feelings and experiences of the past are felt as if the person is reliving it in the present. Abreaction is often embedded in PTSD-- Post Traumatic Stress Disorder. In returning home from war, a soldier might re-experience rather than just remember a past war attack by hiding under a kitchen table when an airplance is heard, screaming for the troop to take cover. With PTSD, the person seems to lose touch with the present when triggered.

Fear of Feeling

What is important to clarify is that supporting a repressed or forgotten memory in surfacing from the unconscious doesn't necessarily release the charge. Feelings can be dissociated so that the client may report it as if it they read it in the newspaper, like it happened to someone else. When negative feelings are not resolved as they happen, they remain very much alive in the energy field and within the body. This indicates that the feelings will need to be made safe to feel or express. Using Creator's teachings while listening to the client's story and digging does help greatly, but it doesn't necessarily create the complete shift right away. It depends on the length of time and the severity of the abuse in how the client starts to fully understand what happened to them.

Many people who have been traumatically abused as children are unable to identify their feelings. Some feelings appear outside the body, completely dissociated. Others are hidden deeply within for protection and safety. There are also feelings that seem frozen, like a freeze frame of energy. Neuro-connections in the brain may not even have certain receptors sites available.

As ThetaHealers®, we know that clients may not understand certain feelings. "What is love? Where is acceptance?" And you cannot get rid of the five basic emotions—joy/happiness, anger, grief/sadness, love, fear. Clients may be told that certain emotions were wrong or bad such as anger or hatred. I have even heard my clients reveal being abused for being too happy as children. Joy and happiness then become shameful and bad.

In reality, all emotions serve us. Denying feelings that are negative doesn't make them go away as mentioned in discussing suppression. All feelings, even ones that appear negative, are worthy of our attention as they can get stuck in our energy field. When we learn to recognize and honor our feelings, and change and forgive the ways we might have acted them out, we will be engaging in a paradigm shift. Our emotions can give us the amazing range to become fully evolved human beings.

There are picture charts on the internet that can be downloaded so that clients with dissociated responses to their feelings can learn to identify what they are feeling.[36]

Even if the emotional charge seems more neutral after the release, there could still be beliefs to clear due to the patterning in the memory and the client's 4th and 5th Plane beliefs. That is why the belief work is essential in moving the client to a higher awareness when they are ready.

Beliefs to test/dig/clear:

◇ My feelings have to be hidden.
◇ Hiding my feelings is the only thing that keeps me safe.
◇ My secrets are greater than my feelings.
◇ I have to hide truth to be safe.

◇ It is unsafe to have all my feeling (this may need to be taught several times if the person has a dissociated disorder until it clears).

◇ I have to take on the feelings of those that hurt me to protect others (family etc).

◇ My feelings have more power than who I am.

◇ The truth took my feelings away.

Creator's teachings:

◇ I understand what my feelings are.

◇ I know what it feels like and how to be safe to have all my feelings at the appropriate time w/o being overwhelmed.

◇ I know what it feels like and how to identify my feelings.

◇ I know when it's safe to have my feelings.

◇ I know what it feels like and how to embody my own feelings.

◇ I know what it feels like and how to separate my feelings from those who hurt me.

◇ I know what it feels like and how to separate my feelings and thoughts from those who were unprotective of me.

◇ I know what it feels like and how to live w/o needing to bury my feelings.

◇ I know what it feels like and how to live w/o needing permission to have my feelings.

◇ I know what it feels like and how to be with my feelings w/o being overwhelmed.

◇ I know what it feels like and how to live w/o secrets.

◇ I know what it feels like and how to have a safe haven for my truth.

◇ I have Creator's definition, understanding and perspective of a safe haven for my truth.

Fear of Being in the Body

> "The truth is incontrovertible. Malice may attack it, ignorance may deride it, but in the end, there it is." –*Winston Churchill*

When a child is abused, the body can be perceived as the betrayer. Children experience their world through their senses in a deep somatic and emotional way. When they are abused, their body can respond to the physical stimulus, perhaps some pleasure or arousal. This becomes extremely confusing and shameful.

The body can also be perceived as dead as the child continues to leave the body to avoid pain and watches above as if the body were an object for others. This action will create huge dissociative responses as the child will lack presence, be unable to track others in conversations, space out frequently, "accidently" run into physical objects, or self-cut to see if they are alive.

When the body is primarily used as an object, its importance is diminished and degraded. Armoring of the body can occur—rigid stance, tightly held in, excess weight for protection, and/or living in only part of the body, usually from the neck up to help the person function on a very mental level (not connecting with the heart or feelings). This creates the appearance that they "look together."

When the body is threatened by abuse and it feels it cannot escape, a 'dissociative' reaction can occur to prepare it for injury. [37] The heart rate and breathing will slow down, and the brain floods with its own painkillers called endogenous opioids causing numbness. This is what happens in an 'out-of-body experience,' or clinically known as 'leaving-the-body sensation' where the child may report watching the events from the outside. This state will return when triggered through a memory, sound, smell or a sight.

The child may appear that they are daydreaming, lose contact with reality, become involved with their inner world to the point that they don't pay attention in class. Teachers' observations may see this as a form of ADHD (Attention Deficit Hyperactivity Disorder) when in reality the child is suffering from trauma symptoms. Psychologists might often misdiagnose the signs of traumatic hypervigilance or dissociation that interferes with the child's attention along with increase of arousal and activity levels. These children actually have a higher than normal neurotransmitters level like noradrenaline (norepinephrine) and adrenaline.

Pain, both emotional and physical, is the regulator of how much the person can be part of their body. **Work on beliefs and give Creator's teachings of protection, safety and strength of the body, and stability and groundedness in being in the body.**

Beliefs to test/dig/clear:

◊ I am only wanted for my body.
◊ My body is the enemy.
◊ I hate my body.
◊ Others (name them) hate my body.
◊ My body betrays me.
◊ My body is dead.
◊ I hold myself together to appear safe.
◊ I am accident prone to know... I'm connected to the world...to remind me I have a body.
◊ I have to leave my body to escape being hurt.
◊ I use my body to hurt myself...to hurt others.
◊ I have to cut myself to know I can feel...that I'm alive.
◊ Pleasure is pain.
◊ Pain is pleasure.
◊ I have to armor my body to protect it from the outside world.
◊ I have to hold tight for the next attack.

◇ I have to be heavy (overweight) to protect myself from others...to be grounded.

◇ It is only safe to be in my head.

◇ I have to die in order to be safe to be alive.

◇ I have to hide my body's vibrancy to be safe.

◇ I have to sell my body to know I'm worthy of anything.

◇ If I shine who I am, I'll be in danger.

Creator's teachings:

◇ I know what it feels like and how to be safe to stay in my body.

◇ I know what it feels like and how to love my body.

◇ I know the difference between pleasure and pain (make sure that their's and Creator's are the same).

◇ I understand my body's amazing strength to survive.

◇ I know what it feels like and how to appreciate my body's amazing strength to survive.

◇ I understand how my body is safe now.

◇ I understand the overall strength of the body in the present.

◇ I understand and know how my body is protected and protects me now.

◇ I know what it feels like and how to be stable and grounded in the body now.

◇ I know that it is safe to be stable and grounded in the body.

◇ I know what it feels like for my body to alive and vibrant.

◇ I know what it feels like to live w/o feeling degraded...w/o feeling my body is degraded.

◇ I know what it feels like and how to be alive w/o thinking of dying.

◇ I know what it feels like to have value as a being human.

◇ I know what it is to value/appreciate my body in the highest and best way.

◇ I know what it feels like for my body to support me in the highest and best way.

◇ I know what it feels like and that's its possible to embrace the beauty of my body.

◇ I know what it feels like to respect my body.

◇ I know what it feels like and how to be safe to shine who I am.

I have also found that assisting the clients in **dialoguing with their body parts** that they resent or hate helps them to somatically release the anger which they turned inward.

> - **Have the client visualize speaking to the body part/s and listening to the response.**
> - **Find out what the client wants or needs from the body part/s.**
> - **Discover what the body wants or needs from the client.**
> - **Negotiate with the body.**
> - **Have the client say something they like about their body each day and keep a journal (ie: I like my blue eyes. I have soft skin).**

Developing respect and acceptance for the body as a consciousness is extremely important for the client and the body. This also opens the way for deep compassion and understanding for oneself.

Fear of/or Anger towards God/Creator

Approximately 90% of our beliefs have to do with our relationship with God/Creator. When an adult is abused as a child, the issues around God become highly charged. In general, since there is a higher correlation in a child knowing the abusing person[38], whether it be the child's parents, relatives, friends of the family, clergy, or teachers, many beliefs come to the forefront about God or Creator as the authority figure who is supposed to protect, show up and be there when needed. This role or identification of God in this way can place the child in an extremely helpless and hopeless position when abused. As a child becomes an adult, the unconscious beliefs permeate the client's relationship in maintaining a paradigm of separation from God/Creator. The client, from that child perspective, often questions:

> *"If God loves me, why would God let this happen to me?"*
>   *(The #1 question that comes up.)*
> *"Where was God in my greatest need?"*
> *"Was God watching me as I was abused? Is God a voyeur?"*
> *"How can I trust a God who doesn't care what happens*
>   *to me?"*
> *"Why would God not stop the abuse?"*
> *"What do I have to do for God to be there for me?"*
> *"Why would I want to be part of a God who would let*
>   *children be so badly hurt?"*

As the practitioner, hold a non-judgmental space for the questions and feelings to arise. You are helping the client to finally verbalize what they have been holding in for years, allowing the anger and grief to surface. You know you are finally coming to a milestone. Here is an example of extracting beliefs from a very common abuse story with just one line. I have had clients say this to me:

"I prayed to God for help but my father would just keep beating me."

You will start to see the beliefs that arise from this in the confusion between God and father. The father represents an authority figure that is very powerful and strong. In a child's perception, with God not answering his/her prayers, it might indicate that the father could be perceived as more powerful than God, that the father is really God, so God is punishing and violent, and that the child will never really have what s/he wants in life so why try or even ask or pray. The person may also think that God becomes selective in who 'It' will attend to and that God will definitely be punitive when and if God shows up at all. There is a profuse hopelessness and anger in the paradigm.

Perhaps the child might try harder to be good so God will show up. The child continues to attempt to prove his/herself worthy of God's attention and acceptance which is projected towards others who might represent authority figures. This is often accomplished through becoming co-dependent and being involved in abusive relationships. The digging process is always a mystery in what directions the client shifts, but after working with abuse for awhile, the patterns will become familiar, and there will be many commonalities that the practitioner will track quickly.

Make sure the client understands the difference between Creator/God-of-All and God of the 5th Plane. This has made all the difference to some of my clients who have been abused and are also Theta practitioners or students.

Beliefs to test/dig/clear:

- ◇ I fear the presence of God.
- ◇ It is unsafe to know God.
- ◇ I resent God for existing.
- ◇ God's existence will make me suffer.
- ◇ God is the authority figure who will punish me.
- ◇ The person who abused me is (or represents) God to me.
- ◇ God is a male.
- ◇ God is a female.
- ◇ I'm unworthy of God's protection...God's safety...God's presence.
- ◇ God will be unable to ever protect me.
- ◇ God abandons me in my greatest hours of need.

⋄ I have to be punished to know God is there.

⋄ If God is really present, I'll be hurt.

⋄ If I pray, I'll be abandoned by God.

⋄ I'm the last on God's list to be helped.

⋄ It is too painful to ask God for anything.

⋄ I'd rather be alone than be connected to God.

⋄ God conspires against me.

⋄ God kills (ascertain what God they really mean).

⋄ I have to work hard to be heard by God.

⋄ God is deaf to my calls for help.

⋄ God is too busy to know I exist.

⋄ I am nothing to God.

⋄ Evil is more powerful than God.

Creator's teachings:

⋄ I know what it feels like and how to live w/o the fear of the presence of Creator-of-All/God in my daily life.

⋄ I know what it feels like to be safe to know Creator-of-All/ God.

⋄ I know what it feels like and how to live w/o suffering...sacrificing...for Creator-of-All.

⋄ I understand that Creator-of-All/God is always sustaining w/o me needing to protect IT.

⋄ I know what it feels like to be blessed by Creator-of-All/ God's presence.

⋄ I know what it feels like to be deserving/worthy of Creator-of-All/God's presence in my daily life.

⋄ I know what it feels like to have Creator-of-All/God's loving acceptance of me.

⋄ I know that Creator-of-All is always there for me in any situation.

⬥ I know the difference between Creator-of-All/God and someone who is a negative authority figure (or someone who hurt me).

⬥ I know what it feels like for Creator-of-All/God to be oneness and wholeness.

⬥ I completely understand, know, realize and feel that Creator-of-All/God is an innate part of who I am.

⬥ I know how to live w/o the fear that Creator-of-All/God punishes me.

⬥ I know what it feels like to be safe/worthy/deserving to pray to Creator-of-All/God w/o feeling abandoned by Creator-of-All/God.

⬥ I know what it feels like to be the precious gift of Creator-of-All/God that I am.

⬥ I know that Creator-of-All/God is always there for me in the highest and best way.

⬥ I know that Creator-of-All/God always has time for me.

⬥ I know what it feels like to be deserving/worthy of Creator-of-All/God's protection.

⬥ I know that I'm a priority in Creator-of-All/God's existence.

⬥ I know what it feels like to be easily heard and listened to by Creator-of-All/God.

⬥ I know that Creator-of-All/God is open to my prayers and questions.

⬥ I understand how Creator-of-All/God is life-affirming.

⬥ I know that Creator-of-All/God's protection is greater than the forces of evil.

⬥ I live with the daily understanding that Creator-of-All/God's protection is greater than any negative force.

The Understanding of Boundaries

Psychological boundaries are symbolic and protective distances between people. On an emotional level, they protect our feelings, thinking and behavior in being responsible, in keeping us separate from others so not to blame others for our behavior or actions. Emotional boundaries can also support us to stop taking responsibility for the feelings, thoughts and behaviors of others.

Physical boundaries enable us to give or refuse permission for others to approach or touch us and for us not to offend others by our advances.

If parents don't teach very young children healthy boundaries, the development can be diminished or arrested. An example could be as simple as a child who is repeatedly told to get up from a seat so an adult can have it. The child's boundaries have been rendered less important (for whatever reason or rationalization of the adult) which can affect the child's sense of esteem and placement.

Spanking is also a violation of a child's boundaries. It is a reactive response by an adult or parent and is invasive to a child, interfering in how s/he functionally interacts in the world.

When children are physically and sexually abused, the concept of boundaries becomes even more impaired. Such boundary violations can often lead to adult victimization through vulnerability to physical battering and rape.

Impaired boundaries can be classified as:

1. **Damaged Boundaries**: Sometimes there is an inability to say "no" in creating safety as well as difficulty between knowing the physical and emotional distance necessary to be safe. The opposite can also be true in using "no" where a "yes" response would work just as well. Control issues can then develop into more serious forms of behavior such as OCD (obsessive-compulsive disorder).

2. **Rigid Wall Boundaries:** Healthy boundaries have a flexibility to them. They can change from day to day depending on the circumstances. What occurs from the effects of physical and sexual abuse is that rigid walls can be put into place instead of healthy boundaries—the use of anger, fear, silence or words (talking on and on) becomes the dominant action to keep distance from others. These behaviors will grow stronger as the child becomes an adult. Walls that once felt protective will hinder the adult from being fully present in most relationships. Boundaries become black or white, life or death, good and bad as reality takes on an edge of ever-present danger whether projected or suppressed.

3. **Lack of identifiable boundaries**: Many adults who have been so severely abused as children are completely unaware of their own or others' boundaries. There is either a tendency to merge, to not be able to separate their behavior or actions from others, or they objectify others so that boundaries are seen as unnecessary and non-existent. It can then become difficult to know the difference between oneself and another.

4. **Vacillation between Rigid Wall boundaries and Lack of Identifiable Boundaries**: With the switching of these defense mechanisms, there is a surrealistic perception of how to operate in the world. The world must be both controlled as well as unrestricted.

One of my clients had gone to her child's high school graduation. The extended family had been invited by the child's father. These relatives had acted in very strange, dissociated ways in the past so that the client had decided to stop communication with them. This was interpreted by the client's estranged sister, who came to the graduation, as being closed-hearted. The client's sister proceeded to shove the palm of her hand, in a pounding motion, between my client's breasts to tell her to open her heart. This seemed natural to her sister, having multiple personalities, as she had also done this to my client's friend as a suggestive measure to share it with my client.

In helping to establish ways for your clients to feel truly safe in their healing of abuse, it is essential to work on the creation of healthy boundaries with them. Be well versed on the subject of healthy boundaries yourself and model that in your relationship with your client. Always ask permission to touch them even if it's only holding their hand or touching their fingers to energy test. Set clear boundaries on your time with them. Letting them call or email you at anytime will not support them establishing the necessary structure of boundaries. Besides, you as the practitioner will start to feel taken advantage of or eventually feel resentful.

It's important to support your client in having healthy sexual boundaries as well. Promiscuity often comes from an impaired understanding of love or self respect, how to receive safe attention from others, and/or a re-enactment of the abuse. You may end up repeatedly supporting your clients throughout the process both with Creator's teachings and counseling them. It's also a good idea to have them read books on co-dependency and healthy boundaries in all kinds of relationships.

If you are actively working with a client who has been sexually abused, it is completely inappropriate to enter into a sexual relationship with them as it will shatter their trust, further damaging their sense of boundaries and healing process, and interferes with the later stages in healing their sexuality. This could also become a legal matter if you are a minister. It is best to end the healing sessions and give space for your own feelings and beliefs to be cleared. Deciding to enter into such a relationship could happen after there has been time to discover the true needs and feelings of both yourself and your client.

Beliefs to test/dig/clear:

- ◇ When others are happy/sad/angry, I also have to be.
- ◇ I'm a victim to others feelings, thoughts, ideas, opinions, actions.
- ◇ I have to act from others' feelings, thoughts, ideas, opinions, actions.
- ◇ I am at fault for the actions of others towards me.
- ◇ I have to be angry/sad/silent/ramble on/blame… to protect myself from others.
- ◇ I have to be alone/escape… to be safe.
- ◇ Saying "no" only makes me feel guilty.
- ◇ I have to say "no" to others to feel myself separate from them.
- ◇ I feel taken advantage if I say "yes" to others.
- ◇ If I have boundaries, I will die.
- ◇ I will unnecessarily restrict how others relate to me if I have healthy boundaries.
- ◇ I have to take on others' feelings to know I'm alive.
- ◇ I feed on others' energy to keep myself alive…safe.
- ◇ It's easier to relate to others who I objectify.
- ◇ Stability only comes when I control my world.
- ◇ I have to control everything around me to know I'm safe.
- ◇ I have to control others to feel sane.
- ◇ I fear losing control of myself resulting in others controlling me.
- ◇ I need to be needed to feel protected.
- ◇ My power is owned by others.
- ◇ I am owned by others.
- ◇ I have to have sex in order to feel_____.
- ◇ I have to refrain from sex to feel safe.
- ◇ I'm safe to show my emotions when I'm sexual.
- ◇ Sex is evil…dirty.

◇ I am a sexual sacrifice.
◇ I have to give up my body to appease others.
◇ I can only feel sexual pleasure if I'm hurt.
◇ I have to stay frozen to be sexual.
◇ I have to be submissive in being sexual.
◇ I have to be dominant in being sexual.
◇ I can never be sexually satisfied.
◇ I use my body as a shield against invasion of others.

Creator's teachings on boundaries:

◇ I have Creator's definition of healthy, flexible boundaries.
◇ I know what it feels like and how to have healthy, flexible boundaries that work for me.
◇ I know what it feels like and how to have healthy boundaries w/o feeling I'm restricting others' actions.
◇ I'm allowed to create boundaries that work for me in the highest and best way.
◇ I know what it feels like and how to respect my own boundaries.
◇ I know what it feels like and how to use my boundaries to protect myself in the highest and best way.
◇ I know what it feels like, how to and when to respect the boundaries of others.
◇ I know what it feels like and how to support myself by creating the boundaries that work for me on a daily basis.
◇ I understand that I can change my boundaries whenever it feels appropriate for me in the highest and best way.
◇ I know how to express what my boundaries are to others in the highest and best way.
◇ I know what it feels like and how to say "no" w/o feeling guilty.
◇ I know how to discern when it feels safe to say "yes" to others' request of me.

◇ I know what it feels like and how to let go of control when appropriate in the highest and best way w/o feeling powerless...w/o feeling taken advantage of...w/o others taking control of me.

◇ I have Creator's understanding, definition and perspective of sanity...stability.

◇ I know what it feels like and how to feel sane/stable on a daily basis.

◇ I know it possible to feel sane/stable w/o needing to control others.

◇ I know what it feels like and how to set time limits in being with others...w/o feeling guilty/selfish/disrespectful.

◇ I know how to live my daily life w/o giving myself away (prostituting myself).

◇ I know how to live w/o giving my power to others.

◇ I know the difference between my feelings/thoughts/beliefs/opinions/ideas/behavior and those of another.

◇ I know how to separate my feelings/thoughts/beliefs/opinions/ideas/behavior and those of another.

◇ I know what it feels like to be connected to myself.

◇ I know what it feels like and how to be connected to others without grabbing for their energy.

◇ I know how to live w/o being a psychic vampire.

◇ I have Creator's definition of interdependency.

◇ I know what it feels like and how to be interdependent... and be safe.

◇ I know what it feels like to be alive and to feel w/o hurting myself in any way.

◇ I know what it feels like, how to and when to be sexual.

◇ I know what it feels like to be safe to be sexual.

◇ I understand how to honor my sexuality w/o feeling the need to give it away.

◇ I know how to feel powerful in the highest and best way while being sexual.

◇ I know what it feels like to feel balanced in how I enjoy being sexual.

◇ I know that Creator-of-All/God protects me when I'm sexual.

◇ I know what it feels like and how to be safe to show my emotions when I'm sexual.

◇ I know how to and when to express my thoughts and truths while being sexual in the highest and best way.

◇ I know what it feels like and how to enjoy being sexual in the highest and best way.

◇ I know when, how, and that I'm allowed to say "stop" when I'm engaging in lovemaking or sex in the highest and best way…w/o feeling upset/guilty/ defensive/angry/afraid.

Betrayal of Trust

A deep-seated form of trauma due to trust being purposely manipulated and abused, particularly for a child who has been physically and sexually abused, is called Betrayal Trauma.[39] It can be at the very core of a person's belief systems. The psychic pain involved in detecting betrayal is an evolved, adaptive motivator for changing social alliances.

When abusive events occur between the child's external reality and his/her social dependence and interactions, it is generally not advantageous for the child's survival to go back for further interaction with those who have betrayed him/her. If the person who has betrayed the child is someone they need to continue interacting with despite the betrayal, ignoring the betrayal and actions would somehow seem essential for their survival.

For a child to withdraw from a caregiver to protect his/herself, whether it be the parents, relatives, teacher, day care provider, clergy, sports instructor, whomever is closely tied to the child, could further threaten the child's life physically, mentally and emotionally. If this pattern of trust betrayal is repeated over and over, by the very nature of this kind of trauma, it would require that the information about the abuse be blocked from the mental processes that control attachment and attachment behavior. It could also create many forms of dissociation including PTSD, attachment disorders and DID/DDNOS.

At 3 years old, Joseph was left for a year by his parents in a foster home that took care of several other children. His parents both wanted to be able to work in order to save money to buy a real home for the family. While being in the care of the husband and wife team, he was abused horrifically by both—tortured, sexually, physically and ritually abused with other children in the home, neglected in dog cages which were guarded by snarling dogs and almost drowned (being hospitalized and even having a Near-Death Experience—NDE). There was no way to escape. This new change in his life left him helpless, defenseless and at the mercy of his caregivers. He made desperate attempts to survive through dissociation and creating a form of attachment disorder. He is still attempting to come to terms with this reality, understand the patterns that have kept him depressed, feeling isolated for most of his life and unable to enjoy intimate, long-term relationships.

Make sure to balance the brain chemistry of your client.

Beliefs to test/dig/clear:

- ◇ I'm afraid of people/adults/authority figures.
- ◇ I hate people/adults/authority figures/children/animals.
- ◇ The world is a dangerous place.
- ◇ I attract dangerous situations.
- ◇ Danger lurks around every corner.

◇ I'm always on guard.

◇ I have to escape from my life (or life, in general).

◇ There is no one to trust.

◇ I trust everyone (also known as victim trust).

◇ If I trust another (can be specific also), I will be abandoned/betrayed/hurt/killed

◇ I have to test everyone for me to trust them.

◇ Life is a testing ground.

◇ I'd rather be alone then connected to others/humanity.

◇ I am clingy when others are around.

◇ It's OK to have needs.

◇ I have to avoid connections with others: to feel a safe space around me/to feel I can handle my life by myself/to keep the secrets.

◇ I'm afraid of any changes in my life.

◇ Change (or the unknown) is devoid of Creator.

◇ Love is always a part of sex.

◇ I go for sex when I want love.

Creator's teachings:

◇ I know what it feels like and how to be safe in every aspect of my life.

◇ I know what it feels like and how to be discerning in the people I connect with.

◇ I know what it feels like and how to be safe with the people I choose to connect with.

◇ I know what it feels like and how to trust the people I choose to connect with.

◇ I know what it feels like and how to trust the people I want to attract into my life now.

◇ I know the difference between victim trust and the discernment in who to trust through Creator-of-All.

◇ I know what it feels like and how to discern what is safe wherever I travel in my life and in the world.

◇ I know what it feels like for the world to feel safe wherever I go.

◇ I know what if feels like and how to discern when situations or places are safe.

◇ I know what it feels like and how to discern a dangerous situation from people who care.

◇ I know what it feels like and how to trust change in my life through Creator-of-All.

◇ I know when to trust change is directed through Creator-of-All and when it's due to my misguided belief systems.

◇ I know how to avoid dangerous situations rather than avoid caring people.

◇ I know how to discern who is an authentically, caring person.

◇ I know what it feels like and how to trust people who really care about me w/o losing my power.

◇ I know what it feels like to be safe to drop my guard and be authentic in expressing myself.

◇ I know what it feels like for my life to be real and matter.

◇ I know what it feels like and how to feel the love for myself rather than being clingy.

◇ I know that it is safe to have my needs met.

◇ I know what it feels like and how to live w/o having to ask permission in order to have what I want in my life.

◇ I know how to ask for what I want in the highest and best way.

◇ I know how to live w/o life needing to be tested.

◇ I know what it feels like and how to be honest with myself in what I need...what I want.

◇ I know what it feels like to give back others' secrets and take my power back.

◊ I know what it feels like and how to live w/o danger being
   my motivator in leading an exciting life.
◊ I know how to see others as Creator-of-All sees them.
◊ I know what it feels like and how allow time and space to
   be intimate with myself (to discovery what I feel).
◊ I know what it feels like and how to discern who is safe to
   be emotionally intimate/physically intimate with.
◊ I know what it feels like and how to be safe to be emotion-
   ally intimate/physically intimate with others.
◊ I know what it feels like, how and when to be emotionally
   intimate/physically intimate with others.
◊ I know the difference between sex and love.
◊ I know the difference between perversion of sex through
   objectification and sex with a loving, authentic connection.

Bonding as Abuse

There is a variance in how the unconscious categorizes or defines
words that may not be in the highest and best way for the client.
Bonding can have its negative side such as the belief:

I am bonded to the perpetrator.

If a child is unable to escape chronic, traumatic abuse, they
will eventually begin to bond with their perpetrator or tormentor.
Whether it be domestic violence, incest, or ritual abuse, they will
feel anxious when alone, and fear abandonment and isolation just
as much as fearing the abuse. The child has not only been a captive to their abuse, but they depended upon their perpetrator for
food, shelter, or other necessities. The perpetrator often plays the
role of the rescuer in appearing to stop the abuse occasionally or
help the child out of the confines of their pain. This comes at a high
price for the child as s/he gives up any freedom with unrelent-

ing loyalty and obedience to the perpetrator. It is derived from a state of powerlessness and regression under situations of extreme stress. This is the foundation of *Trauma Bonding*. It will create a psychological ambivalence and dissociation in a young child. The perpetrator becomes the most powerful person in the life of the traumatized child, and the psychology of the child is shaped by the actions and beliefs of the perpetrator.

Traumatic bonding can be a term applied to battered women who seem unduly devoted to their abusive partners and reluctant to escape, or those who were Holocaust survivors in relying on their guards for their food and sustenance.

Another form of Trauma Bonding is a survival strategy that is often seen in adults held captive, hostaged and/or abused, referred to as the *Stockholm Syndrome*, which is also an emotional bonding with the abuser. It was named after an armed bank raid in Sweden in 1973 when hostages—three women and one man—forged friendly relationships with their captors, even to the point of financing their defense in court and having love affairs with them. Instead of hating the person who has abducted them, they came to empathize with them and view the outside world as the enemy. Even if the person has an opportunity to escape, they will end up staying or defending those that hurt them.[40] This can be exemplified by the case of Patty Hearst who was abducted by the Symbionese Liberation Army in 1974 and became their accomplice, adopting an assumed name and abetting the radical political group in a bank robbery.

Jaycee Lee Dugard, found in Antioch, CA., was eleven when she was kidnapped from her bus stop near her home. She was found after 18 years of captivity where she had been raped, kept outside in sheds, and gave birth to two children. She was completely reliant on her perpetrator and his family for any food or comfort she might have been given. She assisted her abductor with his home business, occasionally greeted customers alone at the door and even went out in public. But she apparently never attempted to escape, returning each day to a shed in the backyard. In looking at the patterns of this type of abuse, it is quite possible that her children had also been abused and held captive so she couldn't leave without abandoning them.

Experts note that because children are especially vulnerable and impressionable, they may be particularly more prone to forming bonds with their captors, a phenomenon that may differ from Stockholm syndrome in adults.

In clearing beliefs on adults who went through these kind of experience as children or adults, it is essential to have the client bring up the beliefs and actions of the perpetrator which is often merged with their own. Have Creator teach them the difference between their beliefs and those who abused them. There may be many. Stay patient and non-judgmental.

Fetal Abuse Healing

Fetuses experience stress and abuse in the womb and can remember their development...ask any adult who has experienced fetal memories or prenatal regressions. There have been scientific studies where fetuses express a biological response indicative of a stress response, and this can happen early in development.[41]

I remember when I was 7 months pregnant with my third child. I was quietly sitting at the kitchen table when my two-year old son threw something on the floor. My tummy got kicked hard by my daughter in my womb in response to the loud noise. Developing fetuses are very sensitive to their environment.

Attempted abortions can and have been remembered by adults

who have survived this trauma. There is a deep feeling of being unwanted, that they should not be here, that they have to fight to live, and that there is not a place for them. This is not mentioned to place guilt or blame if a woman has had an abortion as there is always the Highest Truth in such a decision.

Working with the Inner Child/fetus (having the client nurture the fetus) and belief work in combination with using "Nurturing the Baby in the Womb" exercise helps fetal trauma to heal.

Inner Child/ren Healing

Children will protect themselves in the only ways they can. By cellularly and psychically encapsulating moments of emotional and physical pain and trauma, and by forgetting them (dissociation), the child has the possibility of stopping fear, psychosis or death. As the child becomes an adult, these groupings of split off or dissociated feelings or aspects, create a spectrum of behaviors or conditions that usually do not serve the client any longer. A pattern of coping mechanisms has been developed, and the authentic self, the unwounded, wonder child lies buried under pain and hidden from conscious connection.

The purpose of Inner Child work is really about rediscovering these dissociated feelings or aspects and to become a loving and nurturing parent to oneself through the recognition and rescuing of the Inner Child or Children. It is a re-parenting exercise. One learns to connect to that place inside that is imaginative, wise, mature and caring to help this wounded child accept and reframe the world in a safe new way in the present. Creator's teachings are a supportive supplement to allow the adult to revisit that hidden, seemingly abused Inner Child and make a loving and nurturing connection.

Inner Child Work with one of my clients, "Paul."

Paul had been beaten severely by his father as well as witnessing his mother and siblings beaten regularly. It was a constant war zone with no weapons to fight back. He was always conscious of this and told me that he had spiritually and emotionally done a great deal of work to understand the patterns that recreated themselves through his two marriages. His conversation was geared too much around the patterns, and I could feel that these acknowledgements were intellectual and had no emotional connection.

In scanning his body, I could feel his pattern of emotional holding, the seething and rage that he stored in his liver, the amount of responsibility he carried by himself which showed up in his painful and inflamed shoulder, the parasites in his colon in feeling taken advantage of as well as deep seated resentments, a stiff and painful knee as he felt unable to move forward which was also what he felt as child in being paralyzed by fear, and the lack of support that played out in having to have a hip replacement. As a child, he had attempted to confront his mother in why she didn't stop the abuse or protect herself and all the children. She would cry and then he would feel guilty and retreat.

I was guided to get Paul connected to his feelings and look at more resentments and along with the guilt. I gave him quite a few Creator's teachings to prepare him. I had worked on resentments the session before but realized how deep-seated they were due to his inability to get to his feelings on a somatic level.

I had Paul imagine himself as a young child. I told him to describe what this little boy was wearing and what he was doing. Paul was able to easily drop into this state. I asked if I could hold his hand so he would stay in a Theta state as I watched and guided from the 7th Plane. (It is always a good idea to ask if you can touch someone who was abused. Don't take it for granted.) The little boy was at a distance being afraid and lonely. I suggested that Paul introduce himself to his Inner little boy and ask what the child needed.

"Protection, support and love." That had already been downloaded prior, but the Inner child, in being a split off energy of itself hadn't experienced the change in paradigm even though Paul tested that he knew what these were and he had them through Creator. I find that having the person visualize or imagine a scene is a stronger anchor than fully trusting the finger testing just like in fear digging.

I had Paul ask the child if he would be willing to hold him so he wouldn't be alone and afraid. Paul indicated that the child reached up to him to be held. Having a pre-pubescent daughter, Paul's fatherly instincts took over and he easily walked towards the little boy. He picked up the child and put the boy's little head on his shoulder holding him close. His tears began to flow. I had Creator do more downloads that felt appropriate for this aspect of connection, particularly around regrets of having left this child alone in the past, having kept him abay for so many years, afraid of this child's pain.

Knowing that the Inner child was in safe arms, I asked Paul to imagine his father at a distance. If he needed to have others restrain his father, he was free to imagine this. He visualized two husky men holding his father. I then asked Paul if the child wanted to say anything to the father about all that he had done to him, his siblings and his mother. Paul's Inner child let lose the hatred he had for his father even though this had been pulled and replaced by Creator and what he was obligated to learn. Paul needed to release it through expression. His tone was starting to match the intensity of his feelings. I felt we were really opening up a large release for Paul.

I asked Paul if his father heard him. He said that his father turned his head as if he didn't want to listen to him. I asked Paul what his Inner child wanted to do with the father. "Send him far away."

I suggested a school to learn anger management. Paul's Inner child liked that idea. Paul visualized a bus coming with the two large men carrying the father onto the bus and driving away to the school. I had Creator clear cords between Paul and his father.

I suggested that Paul and his Inner child now visualize his mother from a distance. She didn't need to be restrained as she stood back with her head bowed. I asked the child what he wanted to say to his mother. Paul's voice responded with anger and frustration of how weak she was to not have stopped the abuse, to not protect her children. This was voiced in a less expressive manner than the confrontation with the father. Paul saw that his mother started to cry, which is what she would do when he was little. He felt guilty. (This is the effects of emotional incest where the child takes care of the parent's feelings.) I had Creator do some belief changes and downloads around weakness and strength to clear his feelings around his mother and to grid into these beliefs in order to change his muscle and ligament injuries. His guilt dissipated. He and his child had the mother sent away. I had Creator clear cords and return a soul fragment that he had placed in his mother.

Integration of the energy was needed. I asked Paul where he wanted to place this Inner boy in his body as Paul was holding the child externally. Paul wanted the little boy in his heart. I watched as the child was placed in Paul's heart. Paul's homework was to check in on his child and listen to what the boy needed for about 5 minutes several times per week.

I did a few more downloads and asked him how he was feeling. His painful shoulder felt much lighter and more mobile, his knee wasn't even hurting at all, and he felt lighter and peaceful. I then witnessed a healing from Creator watching the energy go deeper into those injured places.

Paul walked out of the session with a renewed sense of hope, strength, release and a realization of how much he had held in for so many years. Even though he shared that he cried easily at movies, it wasn't about him and what he had gone through. His feelings had been displaced, and now he knew he could feel safer in releasing them without being overwhelmed or made to feel weak. He had a somatic experience in present time of stepping into his true feelings knowing he was actually safe.

Paul's Inner Child experience was very real and empowering to him. Being guided to the Inner child is a loving acknowledgment of the innocence that still exists in each one of us.

Meet your Inner Child Meditation

Just like we have gone on journeys to meet our animal totems in a Theta workshop or gone to a 5th Plane Master in a crystal layout, meeting the Inner Child can be a very profound and touching experience. Many of us have done this kind of work years ago. For those who haven't, consider a new avenue to open your heart. When we become mindful of what may seem like childish needs and hurts, and even the wish to express the unbridled joy which is also there under the surface, we wonder if this would take time away from all the things which seem so important in our adult life. Then, again, what is more important than attending to our deepest needs and feelings or allowing ourselves to cry those unshed tears that have been waiting for expression for years? What is more important than expressing childlike exuberance? We don't just find our unmet needs and past hurts when we connect with our Inner Child... we also find a source of our joy.

There is a beautiful meditation by Louise Hayes that brings tears to my eyes even though I've done years of Inner Child work in the past and felt I didn't really need it any longer. I invite you to take 5 minutes to listen to it at the footnoted website.[42]

[**For teachers:** You can also read the below section to your students in a slow, loving and compassionate voice that will bring up their feelings and soften their heart. Take your students up to All-That-Is. Have them feel the peace, calmness and centeredness that is in this connection.]

To be spoken to students or client:

Visualize yourself welcoming the child that you were. Put your hand over your heart and allow yourself not only to see your Inner Child but to be that child. Let my voice be your family as I say to you:

We're so glad you came. We've wanted you so much to be part of our family. You're so important to us. We're so glad that you're such a wonderful little boy (or little girl). We love your uniqueness and specialness. The family wouldn't be the same without you. We love you. We want to hold you. We want to help you grow up to be all that you want to be. You don't have to be like us. You can be yourself. You're so beautiful. You're so bright. You're so creative. It gives us such a pleasure to have you here. We love you more than anything in the whole world. We thank you for choosing our family. We know you are blessed. You have blessed us by coming. We love you. We really love you.

Let your little child make these words true for it. Be aware every day that you can say these words, and you can hold yourself. You can look in the mirror and say these words. You can have a friend hold you and say these words.

Tell yourself all the things you wanted your parents to tell you. Your little child needs to feel wanted and loved. Give that to your child no matter how old you are or how sick or how scared. Your little child needs to be wanted and loved. Keep telling your child that, *"I want you and I love you. It is the truth for you. The Universe and Creator-of-All want you here and that's why you are here. And your Soul wants you to be here too. You've always been loved and will always be loved. You can live happily, and so it is."*

The Continuum of Dissociation

A person can have one Inner Child that looks like the age of the child at each occurrence of abuse, or many Inner Children due to dissociative disorders of severe, sadistic abuse and torture, known as Dissociative Identity Disorder (DID), or Dissociative Disorder Not Otherwise Specified (DDNOS).[43] Consider that the Inner Child might be described as stuck in an emotional freeze frame that seems held in the past if not healed.

Dissociation is a common coping mechanism not only of abuse but in life in general. Everyone dissociates at times, from driving a car on a familiar route and not consciously remembering how you got there, to spacing out in front of the TV, to being unable to track a conversation because you are thinking about what happened to you hours before. And the Grand Dissociation is thinking we are separate from Creator-of-All. But not everyone has a dissociative disorder. I have heard professionals say that we all have multiple personalities.[44] I do not agree with this assessment. There is a big difference between having multiple personalities and having sub-personalities (the critic, the judge etc.), all of it a part of being multi-dimensional.

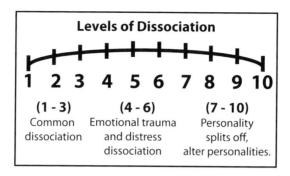

There are varying levels of dissociation. A simplified way of understanding this complex phenomenon is to picture an arc. On the left hand side is the common dissociation and forgetfulness which "#1 to 3" represent- everyone forgets at times and then later remembers things and events. The farther we go to the right of the continuum, however, the more the person is apt to dissociate at times of emotional trauma and distress. This is represented as "#4 to 6." If the abuse escalates to severe trauma, personality parts split off creating fragments or sometimes alter personalities.[45] There is a loss of consciousness among the alters with the host (core) personality. This is considered "#7 to 10" on the continuum.

Working with Inner Children or alters from such a creative coping mechanism will not be covered in any depth as it is much more complicated. In general, though, I use some of the same methods described in this workbook but geared specifically for working with large groups of dissociative parts. The most important support a practitioner can give for these clients is to help them feel safe, discover their parts, and then get the parts in conversations and negotiations among each other. This process of co-consciousness opens up the amnesiac barriers within the mind that holds the memories and the parts so very separately.

Each alter has a job within a system or systems which has to do with protecting the host, body or memory. It is important to ascertain what each alter is responsible in doing; and when there are hundreds of parts, it's good to establish system leaders for internal communication. Having the parts work together as a cohesive unit/s are what help to create stability and functionality for the client. Integration occurs when the host personality is feeling deep love for the alters and him/herself, and/or as the alters jobs and positions are no longer necessary for survival.

Complete integration or fusion (merging into a one personality state) is not the goal. When it happens, it is very divinely orchestrated. In all honesty, I personally feel that it is ideal when the person (host personality), the alters, and the Spirit/Soul feel they are ready for their next evolutionary step. Life doesn't have to be so separated or difficult. I've spoken with people with DID who say they feel quite functional in keeping their "inside people" as they are. I've also witnessed the complete fusion of personalities in several clients, all who felt readiness to be in the world in a new way.

Healing is a continual evolution of consciousness. Why stop the healing to stay separated when there exists other possibilities of reality that are easier and less of a struggle? That's where working on the 5th Plane beliefs and programs support a new paradigm to actually emerge completely.

Approaching a client about what you "see" intuitively

> **"All great truths begin as blasphemies."**
> – *George Bernard Shaw*

Your connection with Creator-of-All will guide you to disclose if you intuitively "see" repressed abuse memories. Sometimes Creator will tell you that the client is not ready to know and sometimes the client already suspects or knows but just hasn't disclosed to anyone.

Many years ago, I had a client who had a deep pain in her neck. When I scanned it, I saw an alien implant. I had Creator change it and completed the scan. I asked the client how she was doing. She said her neck felt way better. What had I done?

I didn't want to stir up anything at the time so I just said that it wasn't important. At which she commented, "Did you take an implant out?" To say the least, I was surprised, but I answered her honestly as she already knew.

In the case where the client doesn't remember but you sense it is time to move them along, gently share that you suspect something happened to them that they may not remember which is affecting their action in the world. As I've mentioned before, I often see a cloud of energy that seems to be masking their deeper beliefs. (The releasing core beliefs lie within or under the cloud.) So again, the belief work will not fully get to the issue because the beliefs are layered within or under the memory energy.

A client can start to feel suspicious of hidden abuse/trauma because of other family members sharing about their remembering of being abused, or the client has been told by other psychics but just doesn't have any concrete memories. Nightmares can sometimes be repressed memories as mentioned before.

When I work with a client who I suspect was abused, I slowly bring up the topic by using the energy testing to reveal the clients beliefs once they feel safe. I make sure they know that the finger testing can be indicative of the body, mind and spirit wisdom on four levels. I want them to know that 88% of their beliefs are at a subconscious level so even if they don't remember something, it's a good possibility that it's hidden deep down. Is this not true in our understanding of working with beliefs?

Sometimes, though, the client's psyche isn't ready for certain information and will give you an opposite energy testing than what you are seeing or sensing in your connection with Creator. Attempt not to doubt yourself. You may actually be picking up the feelings and trepidations of the client as you scan. Information can be layered as mentioned before. I have seen clients test "no" to abuse only to remember abuse several years later. You are being 'signaled' to continue supporting the "remembering" in being safe and not rushing things.

Also, check to make sure that the client is in their body when testing. Talking about the possibility of exploring abuse can have them use the coping skill of exiting (dissociation). It might be helpful to say, "I notice you slightly above your body. Would you like to be more present and we can energy test more accurately?" If they agree, have Creator return them and use downloads to help them feel safe.

Use your wording wisely. Instead of having them test, "I was molested when I was 4", you could say, "I see that it looks like something happened to you when you were 4. Are you ready to know the truth about your history? Can we test some beliefs around this?" If the client gives permission, you might test, "I was touched inappropriately at 4." It's a gentle approach and easier for the client to handle.

Ask them repeatedly during their session or continuing sessions if they feel safe in exploring and knowing their history and truth. Empower them so that they can feel that their truth is wise and safe, and that whatever happened, they already lived through it.

I often hear:

"Do I have to remember what happened?"

"Can't we leave well-enough alone?"

"Why would I want to know if something horrible happened to me?"

"The past is the past. How can I be in the present if we bring up the past?"

"This could be a past life…right?"

And my answer will be close to the following: *"You don't have to know, but if it is there, it is holding up your energy. To forget takes more energy than remembering. It's like a pressure cooker stored up and affecting you. You will eventually know if it's true. You will feel it in your body and in your emotions as it releases. Creator will not reveal more than you can handle. You have a right to know your true history. It's fear and your timing that is keeping you from claiming your truth and the reality of your life. I can help you work with your fears."*

Your tone and expression can greatly ease your client's anxiety as well. If the client is seeing you in person, ask if you can hold their hand (like in Paul's story) and keep your eyes focused gently on them. Keep your breath even. Be authentic and compassionate. They can tell if you are faking it. And don't act afraid under any circumstance. You are holding a very safe space for them to reveal. They want to know that you can handle whatever they tell you. This would also be true in Creator showing you their memories. You are there to support the unveiling of Truth.

If the client is reluctant to know more, gently question, **"What's the worse thing that would happen if what you suspected were true?"** and **"How will the truth change your life?"** Use these questions to dig out issues that will eventually make them safe to remember.

Beliefs to test/dig/clear:

◇ I'm unsafe to know my truth.

◇ Creator's truth is unsafe.

◇ My truth is unsafe.

◇ I will never be safe.

◇ Truth has to be difficult...hidden.

◇ Truth separates me from _____ (my family, loved ones, children, God, my parents etc).

◇ My family (mother, father, siblings, relatives, etc.) will reject/abandon/kill me if I know the truth.

◇ I have to protect my family from the truth.

◇ Denial is easier than truth.

◇ Truth is lies.

◇ Lies are truth.

◇ I will die if I know the truth about my history.

◇ Secrets keep me safe.

◇ I have to keep the family secret to continue to belong to my family.

◇ I have to protect my family from my secret or they will be hurt.

◇ I'm hiding a secret to protect my family (or whomever).

◇ I have to protect my family from my secret or I will disappear.

◇ I need permission to remember the truth.

◇ Love is abuse.

◇ I can only receive the love in my family if I receive the abuse.

Creator's teachings:

◇ I know what it feels like, how to, and when to be open to the truth of my life through Creator-of-All.

◇ I know the truth of my life through Creator.

◇ I know what it feels like and how to be safe to know the truth through Creator.

◇ I know what it feels like and how to be safe to remember what happened w/o reliving it.

◇ I know what it feels like and how to handle the truth in the highest and best way.

◇ I know what it feels like and how to integrate the truth in the highest and best way.

◇ I know what it feels like and how to align the truth of my life with Creator's truth and feel safe.

◇ I know what it feels like and how to separate what happened in the past from the present.

◇ I know what it feels like for Creator to protect me as I remember the truth of my life's history.

◇ I know how to live without needing permission to remember my life's history.

◇ I know it's OK to remember what happened to me.

◇ I know that Creator is always with and a part of me no matter what happened to me.

◇ I know the difference between truth and lies.

◇ I know what it feels like for Creator to make my truth safe.

◇ I know what it feels like and how to trust Creator to make my truth safe.

◇ I know what it feels like and how to stop protecting my family's secrets and know my own truth aligned with Creator's truth.

Memory Retrieval- How to Proceed

It's a good idea to check for and send all entities and waywards to Creator's Light. There is no need to have interference. Sometimes entities won't release until a memory is also released so be aware.

When the person is ready to proceed in releasing the memory, make sure that you take them up in Theta to the 7th Plane. Even though I'm also a clinical hypnotherapist, I use the ThetaHealing® Meditation to take my clients into a trance state to experience a connection with Creator-of-All. Once at the 7th Plane, have them repeat the command that they hear from you.

> *"Creator-of-All, it is commanded that I be shown what happened to me as a child that is causing my fears or symptoms. Thank you, it is done (3x)"*

Guide them in feeling, seeing, hearing, sensing what happened. From the 7th Plane, this makes things go more smoothly unless they are afraid of Creator. If they are afraid, you can test the beliefs on pages 37 to 39 or just start doing the fear work on them, but often these particular fears are based in releasing the abuse memory. In this case, just let them be in a Theta state through their connection with you being at the 7th Plane.

If they started the release of the memory without you taking them to the 7th Plane, they are in a Theta brain state already. Pace and track them using the questions from the crystal layout and digging session awareness (where, what, how, when, who, why) as suggested on the following page. These questions are appropriate whether or not the client is fully connected at the 7th Plane. Just make sure that you, as the practitioner, are connected.

- Where are you?
- What does this place look like?
- Is it familiar?
- How old are you?
- What are you wearing?
- Are you alone or are there others with you?
- Who is with you?
- What is happening?
- What are you feeling? (keep checking in with this question)
- Where do you feel this in your body?
- What happened next?

Continue with these questions to prompt and guide them to remember. Allow for any emoting and tell them that they are safe and it is present time. You do not want them to abreact if possible (a sense of reliving it in the past) which often happens in PTSD or DID. As you listen to their story, supplement with Creator's teachings that seem appropriate.

The body is a great indicator of tension and expression of what happened as the feelings of abuse become registered in the body. If all of a sudden the client feels tension in their vagina or their jaws feel tight, ask the client to give it a number from 1-10 of intensity and check back later if this tension level has dropped and at what number they would consider it. I like to support the client in getting to "1", which means "none." You can command to remove memory imprints (command to release cellular trauma, and watch the cells release) if there is an increase of physical pain from or during the memory.

Make sure that the client returns to an even breathing if they start to hyperventilate or decrease their breathing pattern. Checking for and removing Free Floating memories (Engram banks) that might have been created from the abuse is important. Allow time for the client to continue to remember.

One memory may have a vast amount of information. Some people go into a great deal of detail as they are in a Theta state describing everything they see, hear, or feel. This is appropriate and verifying for the client because the details make it more difficult to deny. Why would they make all this up? (unless, of course, they are schizophrenic, and sometimes this can be based in childhood abuse). The memory may also have interconnecting parts that go off in several tangents. In both cases, the memory may need to be limited by the time of the session. It's important that the Inner Child be rescued or taken to a safe place and then placed within the body even if the memory hasn't been fully completed. The goal is safety and empowerment.

Memory Retrieval Basic Steps

- **Remove entities, waywards or demonic energies.**
- **Take client to 7th Plane.**
- **Have them repeat command to themselves.**
- **Have them and yourself shift consciousness to what happened (track them).**
- **Ask the client questions and clear fears.**
- **Check in on the tension in their body to reduce it.**
- **Remove memory imprints, cellular trauma and Free Floating memories.**
- **Do Inner Child Rescue and have client place child in their body.**
- **Check in.**
- **Bring client back through body, grounded, disperse energy in body and do break.**
- **Command for integration and do healing.**
- **Give homework for client to check in with Inner Child.**

The Rescue

When the abuse has been revealed to the level it can be for that session, then this is the time to **"Rescue the Inner Child."**

1) Have the adult self or a person who the client feels is strong and protective, like a super hero, Inner Parent, or Creator, take the Inner Child to a very safe place. Sometimes it does occur that the adult self feels incapable of being responsible for the Inner Child as there is a blending of feelings. This is the best situation for the use of alternative beings.

2) Have the client describe the rescue and the safe place in detail.

3) See if the client will hold the Inner Child or if the Inner Child will let the client hold them. (I have seen the Inner Child not want the adult to get close and visa-versa.)

4) Have the client ask if the Inner Child needs anything. Perhaps the child wants the person to believe him or her. Perhaps the child wants a warm healing bath.

5) Have the client dialogue with the Inner Child. If the client is resistant in talking to the Inner Child, ascertain their feelings and change their beliefs so that a connection can occur.

6) You can have the client mock up the abusive person at a distance. If the child is afraid of being attacked, make sure that the adult or child imagine a strong person/s to restrain the perpetrator.

7) Ask the client: "What would the child like to <u>say</u> to this person who hurt you?" Have the child express his/herself to the perpetrator, outloud in first person, in front of you. They might want to scream at the person (you can mock up that scene like

I did with Paul). They might want to punch the perpetrator. Allow them to move their arms or legs as the energy will flow out. This is all appropriate. You can just have Creator clean it up.

Do not have judgment if the client wants to kill the person in the inner world who hurt them. Rage and anger are appropriate in a contained sacred space...in fact, it can be totally transforming as people have used this energy against themselves or others rather than acknowledging, feeling or releasing it. Know that you are safe as a practitioner unless Creator is telling you differently (which would happen way before you got to this point). *I have never been physically attacked by a client except once and that was only because an entity was there. As vertically challenged as I might appear, my strength of restraining that client worked fine as I had Creator pull the entity out. I was not afraid at all as I trusted Creator was orchestrating the entire session.*

If the expression is dull or flat, coach the client to match the tone with the feeling. Sometimes this takes more than one session because the client has never been empowered to verbally express him/herself and the feelings are so dissociated.

I have worked with my clients in doing some breathing exercises that allow for an emotional release along with Creator's teachings.

Breathing exercise:

- Stand next to the client if the client is sitting or sit in front of the client. I have had my clients do this exercise even if we were connected by phone. I just let them know that I'm right there with them and they can hear this in my voice.

- Ask if you can either hold their hand or touch their shoulder if in person. Being witnessed is very important as most abused children never had anyone safe to tell or were afraid to reveal. Their pain was held alone.

- Have the client breathe from their gut to their mouth allowing noise or sound to release. Make sure that they keep their mouth open. If necessary, breathe with them to help pace them. Have them make the sound louder. You might also have them breathe out "no" or "don't you touch me."

- Anger may eventually release to tears. Stay present and keep telling them that they are safe and doing great. This expressive release helps to clear levels of stuck energy so beliefs can now be verbalized and changed.

8) Ask the client, "What would the child like to <u>do</u> with this person who hurt you?" The imagination of the client is wonderful at choosing how to distance themselves from the abusive person. They might send them to the North Pole or to God's light. This is very empowering for the client.

9) Have the client visualize placing the Inner Child in their body. This is a good time to return soul fragments (in the highest and best way for this time...you don't want to flood them with memories)...and have psychic hooks or cords returned or released.

10) Check in with how they feel, and use downloads that are appropriate for how they are feeling.

11) Bring the client back to the 7th Plane if they are not there or down above the crown for rinsing and drying off of the consciousness and then through the body to the middle of the earth. Bring grounding energy back up to the crown and let it disperse. Show them the Huna break and zip up.

12) Give the client a homework assignment to touch base with the Inner Child so they know that they are loved, heard, felt and cherished. Use downloads to support this. You are teaching the client how to re-parent themselves, to develop love and compassion for all that they are. You are bringing them into the present.

Not every session that you facilitate with people who were abused is about memory retrieval. Support the client to make recommendations on what they want in the sessions. Sometimes just a listening ear and some Creator's teachings is all that is needed and wanted. It takes time to process deep memories for some. And like I've said, other people move through it quickly depending on how severe and how long it went on.

Verifying Emerging or Recovered Memories

> "Even if I am a minority of one, truth is still the truth."
> – *Ghandi*

Oftentimes, clients want some way to verify their feelings or memories that surface. Having the client discuss possible abuse or memories with their families, family friends or associates can sometimes be risky and needs to be done carefully, if at all, especially if the family is in any way involved with the abuse. Inquiries can be threatening to some family structures. As a practitioner, you can feel this in what the client discusses and clears during their belief sessions.

If the family was like a war zone or secretive when the client was growing up, there is probably a great deal of denial and little safety for the client to really share the truth with their family unless the family has done work on themselves. Recovering memories can break the family rules of "no talk" to confuse the truth of the client as well as the protecting the person who harmed the client as a child. Discretion is important. Check in with Creator.

Sometimes the family wasn't involved but personal denial and religious beliefs keep them from believing the client.

Examples: *"A priest couldn't have done such a thing to you. You are a sinner for saying that."* Or *"Grandpa would never hurt you. I never left him alone with you."* Or *"The past is the past. It's over. Get over it whatever it is."* Or *"I knew you always wanted to get back at the family and now you are doing it."*

These situations can create the client to doubt themselves and attempt to measure their truth against their families' skepticism or denial. You might ask them how it serves them or their family to continue this pattern as a way to dig this out.

The client needs to develop a strong and stable internal structure of truth and support (positive ego strengthening) before "confrontation" or truth verifying is ever suggested. It's important to support the client to know their truth through themselves and through Creator.

Ways clients can verify memories:

- Ask Creator.

- When appropriate, collaborate with family members, neighbors, family connections, friends and the police.

- Corroborating data: scenes remembered during a memory show up as real; feelings around holidays or special events that start to change after remembering; songs that come up during a memory that were forgotten; names appear that the client didn't remember consciously and can be verified; medical record verification.

Patterns of Awareness: Supporting the client in believing his/her own memories:

There are some specific patterns that emerge as memories are recovered. With the practitioner being aware of them, s/he will be able to support the client to feel validated in what has surfaced.

- If the client has a great deal of emotional pain and the memories seem to fit the pattern of the pain they are in, then the memories are likely to be valid. If the client is emoting heavily saying *"This couldn't have happened. Why would the person do such a thing!"* this is not the time to become analytical in your response. Question gently, *"Do you think you would be crying hysterically if nothing happened?"* Give time for the feelings to integrate or give some downloads to calm the person down.

- Waves of doubt often occur right after a memory surfaces or when shared with unsupportive family members.

- The client will get angry when people don't believe them, but doubt that it's true when someone does believe them.

- Notice the kind of emotional or physical symptoms the client had before a memory and if that changes afterwards. If it does, it's a good indicator of the release and this could be mentioned to the client.

- Clients who have been abused rarely seek out comfort for their pain and feel undeserving of it when given. Asking for a hug or asking to be held is difficult. This signifies that the memory work is most likely real.

- A client is often worried that every detail might not match what happened or not be completely accurate. Reinforce that this doesn't even happen with conscious recall.

- For clarity, discuss with the client how their parents, family members etc. reveal patterns of trauma responses that are symptomatic of abused children as well.

- If other siblings report having similar fears or symptoms as the client, this is good to point out.

- The family may have fabricated stories in the past that the client is consciously aware of. Bring this to the client's attention.

- Have the client compile a list of ongoing confirmations of truth. Explain to them that this is more important than focusing how the memory couldn't be true.

It's important to realize that even after the client accepts what has happened to them, there are many patterns and beliefs that need to be cleared.

Clearing the Ancestral Lineage that Holds Abuse Patterning

If a client's abuse occurred within the confines of the family and the abuse seems to pattern back into past generations, it is a good idea to check their beliefs on an ancestral level. This is best done once a client has worked on clearing trauma and beliefs held on a personal core level.

What does this mean? Clearing out the perceptions of how a person's ancestors might think on a subject in relationship to the client's life will help clear out the genetic lineage in getting to deeper levels of genetic beliefs. The ancestors' memories are held in the client's cells so their body will respond to it most often as a separate program.

Perhaps the client has cleared the beliefs that *"I am free from secrets."* Have the client imagine what their ancestors might say about this. Ask them:

"What is your perception of your ancestors' feelings about this topic? How do you think they would have thought about it?"

You might surprisingly hear responses such as:

⬦ My ancestors are slaves to their secrets.
⬦ My ancestors have to keep secrets to keep honor.
⬦ My ancestors have to hurt others to protect themselves
⬦ My ancestors have to hide the truth to protect the family lineage from collapsing.

There could be many beliefs of a similar nature depending on how the client's session is being directed by Creator. In the wording, you can specify a particular person in the ancestral line (i.e. *"My Great-Uncle Robert keeps secrets to keep honor"* or *"My Grandmother Rose has to hurt others to protect herself"*), but just stating "my ancestors" will usually cover the entire genetic line.

Remember that the unconscious mind will compartmentalize words of similar meaning. Besides clearing anger, hatred and resentments, check how your client might be offended by their ancestors such as below.

◇ I am offended by my ancestors' behavior...actions.
◇ I have to be offended to be safe from my ancestors (keeps distance).
◇ I have a duty/responsibility to clean up my ancestors to free the future generations.
◇ I have to free my genetic lineage to change the future generations.
◇ To play my role in the family, I have to be everyone's dumping ground...savior...protector...martyr (fill in the blank).
◇ It's weak to call in assistance in healing my genetic lineage.

Creator's Teaching:

◇ I understand how Creator is a part of my genetic lineage.
◇ I know what it feels like, how to, and that it's possible for Creator to change my genetic lineage in the highest and best way.
◇ I know how Creator participates in my genetic lineage.
◇ I allow Creator to participate in changing my genetic lineage.
◇ I know what it feels like and how Creator supports the change in my genetic lineage in the highest and best way.
◇ I know what it feels like and how Creator is protective of my genetic lineage w/o supporting its dysfunctional behavior.
◇ I know how to participate in my genetic lineage w/o allowing others to dump on me...without being a savior... without having to protect their dysfunctional actions... without being a martyr.
◇ I know what it feels like and how to have (or ask for) support

from others...from Creator... in the healing/change of my genetic lineage.

Curses often run in ancestral lineages such as a generational curse. These can be cleared as discussed in the Basic ThetaHealing® textbook (page 165). It's important to remember that such psychic attacks come in through the beliefs of guilt and the deserving of punishment. When a client has been abused, these beliefs are often held strong, particularly if the person has been ritually abused.

Interestingly, 'blessings' are much stronger than curses in the way they energetically tie a person to another situation or person. In a negative sense, it can be like an infusion of the client's energy that becomes counter-productive for them. As irrational as it may seem (most beliefs are irrational but none-the-less, protective), a client may have a beliefs that:

◇ I am blessed by my ancestors keeping secrets.

◇ It's a blessing to have my ancestors hide the family situation.

> **You can easily clear these programs just like an obligation by going to the 7th Plane and witness it cleared through all four levels. If it doesn't clear, dig down and find the lesson.**

Heart Song Exercise

In just being born, we pick up the imprint of everything that has happened on the planet besides the ancestral, genetic and past life memories that we carry with us. If we were then victimized through physical and sexual abuse in this life, there is the addition of traumatic memories. To help release old sorrow, anguish, pain and anger, have your client practice the Heart Toning with you assisting or by themselves (make sure they know how to use the map to All-That-Is). This exercise allows the sound that is locked in the heart to express through the mouth and completely release. The vibration of sound shouldn't be high or too low.

It is best for this exercise to continue until all the negative, built-up feelings are released from the heart and other body parts whether it happens in one session or over a period of time. The client will just feel finished, with a sense of joy and laughter available different than before.[46]

Creator's Teachings:

◇ I know what it feels like and how to be safe to make a difference.

◇ I know what it feels like, how to, and when to make a difference in any situation.

◇ I know what it feels like to acknowledge and accept that everything I've experienced counts/matters.

◇ This time, things count/matter.

◇ I know what it feels like, how to, and when to wake people up to their potential.

◇ I wake people up to their potential.

Forgiveness

Though forgiveness is such an important spiritual principle, it cannot be rushed at all when deep traumatic abuse is involved. It is true that all the people who might have acted within the context of the abuse must eventually be forgiven/released, but it is in the client's timing, their soul journey. Pushing it can make the client feel guilty, ashamed, self-blaming and resistant. It can slow down their process to integrate what happened to them and find peace and completion.

The most important forgiveness is towards oneself. The ways we have acted towards ourselves, repeating patterns of self abuse or sabotaging, is essential to recognize and clear. Learning to release toxic shame[47] and self hatred, and regaining self-love, self respect and self-acceptance is such a large part of the healing.

With deep trauma, forgiveness towards oneself or others doesn't happen all at once due to the layers of what really happened in the person's life. How can you forgive someone if you don't even know what they did to you? How can you forgive yourself if you don't remember the ways in which you acted in self-sabotaging actions due to fear of remembering what happened? And when you do remember what others did or what you did to yourself or others, what if it completely changed the reality of your life so much so that you felt the foundation of your life was crumbling, that your life was a fake and that you made up a story to appease others and to protect yourself from what really happened? That is a great deal to integrate!

On several occasions, I have worked with clients whose abuse memories surfaced as the incidents happened only once or twice; and they cleared completely along with the associated feelings with the ability to forgive themselves and who hurt them in one hour. This is the exception, not the rule.

Forgiveness is the highest form of protection and, in Truth, just means that the lessons in what the person/people/situation have done hurtfully to the client, including the client to him/herself, have been completely processed to the point where release and compassion flow naturally. The highest overview has been experienced.

When the client is ready, a wonderful practice is to support them in saying both to themselves, and to the abuser/s through thoughts, *"I forgive you."* From the client's heart, by repeating in cycles of three, *"I forgive you,"* it will tell the abuser energetically, *"This is done, and I'm not giving you any more of my energy. You can't have any of my anger, grief or feelings. This will never happen again, and I am standing up for myself."* By saying, *"I forgive you,"* the projected negative energy coming from another dissolves or goes through the person who was abused either to the Creator-of-All or back to the abuser.

Anything that brings our energy down doesn't have the right to continue. The abuser/s that you or your client are giving your energy to in hating, resenting, being angry at, or holding a grudge against just doesn't deserve your energy, and it allows them to stop your internal progress. By simply forgiving them in the truest sense, you'll stop giving them any more energy and be able to have the power returned to you that is rightfully yours.

Even for people who have been severely abused with the perpetrator having had power over them for many years, by saying through thought, *"I forgive you,"* could help free them from giving energy to the abuser/s. They might want to consider doing this one or two times even if it's a difficult practice. The goal is for the abuser to stop having any participation in their life.

For ThetaHealers®, if you spend time being angry at the abuser, it could be the one thing that is going to stop you from instant healings on yourself or from being abundant. Why should the abuser have that much power over you?

Creator's teaching:

   ◇ I know what it feels like and how to forgive things, people, and situations from the past that are taking my energy now.

   ◇ I know what it feels like, how to, and that it's possible to feel completely protected through forgiving another.

   ◇ I know how to tell the difference between what I did that caused harm to another and what another did that caused harm which I took on as my own.

   ◇ I know when the process of forgiveness is complete.

Forgiveness Steps

- **Find out why the client (or you) resent the person.** (They won't keep the feeling unless they think it will protect them in some way.)
- **Find out what they learned from the abuser/ situation.**
- **Teach them that they can learn something good without another abusing them.**
- **Free the client (or yourself) from the obligation of being abused.**
- **Then have them add "I forgive you," 3 times.**

Remember that if it's repeated repressed abuse memories, you may be going over the forgiveness process many times until the client has released a good portion of the memories to get to real forgiveness. That's why I find that the addition of Inner Child work allows a somatic expression of empowerment so forgiveness/release can come quicker.

I will never forget a past client, part Native American, who had advancing lung cancer. He was 50, and every generation of men in his family (father, grandfather, brother) died at 50 years old. He had just turned 50 when I met him. He didn't want chemotherapy or radiation. He had decided that I would be his 'healer'.

I talked to Vianna about him, and she said, "He has 26 resentments. Good luck!" I felt I had been given a challenge and decided I was up for it.

Over the four months I worked with him, as I did digging, downloads, and Inner Child work, his life story started to unravel very severe childhood trauma by multiple family members and friends of the family. It is the reason he had abused himself in the past by his addiction to heroin, alcohol, and cigarettes.

We discovered three dissociated Inner children; and during our time in session, he made deep and loving connections with them. He had an eight year old son so his fatherly love shifted easily in connecting to these three inner boys. After several months, the little boys decided that women were no longer safe to work with as memories of maternal sexual abuse arose, and he grew weaker and weaker. He did not get to clear all those 26 resentments because he didn't have the time to discover all the people who were involved in his abuse. He ended our professional relationship though I checked in on him through email. He was part of my soul family, and I loved him.

He also had a male therapist who supported him during and

after we parted and had actually sent him to me initially. Due to the extent of the repressed trauma and his past addictions, his body could not continue even though he told me that memories continued to come. He died three months later.

I rarely feel the grief now, only when I write about him. He broke my heart open in such expansive ways that it's hard to put words on the feelings...lessons of love and forgiveness through thousands of years. I cleared 25 past lives with him, and he never knew it while physically on this earth.

Moving Beyond Abuse

As release/ forgiveness occur, this is a good time to remove and release cords that were unconsciously placed between the client and those who harmed the client.[48] When release is complete, there is no more fear in seeing the abusive person though the client may choose to stop all connections due to personal discernment of safety and the ongoing evolution of their soul. Forgiveness is not about forgetting what happened or condoning the abuse. It is always interesting that people will accept disrepsect and/or abuse from family members or in business that they would never allow in friendships. One does not need to be put themselves in a situation for possible re-abuse to feel compassion and love for all that has been learned. Learning to respect oneself and one's boundaries is a huge evolutionary shift for those who were once abused.

In the client's decision to stop further contact with certain factions of their life, there is no longer an anchor of wanting to keep denial in place by needing to take care of or protect the family and/ or the abuser. Even if certain family members or friends weren't directly involved with the client's situation, there are often feelings of discomfort when facing the reality of what can happen in families where abuse occurs. It is not unusual that these people will lobby for the "norm"—the old adage that "families must stick together" even if they continue dysfunctional and harmful patterns. People who have released their parents, families and friends due to abuse deserve the utmost respect and support.[49] They have risked it all to heal, to know and live from their own truth. They exemplify a deep inner conviction which supports others to discover their strength, to live their truth and be in integrity to themselves.

If the client would not put themselves in danger by being with the person/s who s/he was abused by as a child and feels that they want to either be in or continue a relationship, this is between the client, the one who had been abusive and Creator.

Check beliefs on the client of how the relationship would serve them, what they feel they would get out of it, how would it support them and the other person, and what expectations they might have about the connection. Make sure that issues of guilt, promises, contracts, trades, and obligations are worked on and completed.

I have seen adults who wanted to say goodbye, in person, as their once abusive parent was dying. It was a profound completion as they could hold a space of love and compassion in all that they learned from this person during their life. It was a new beginning for them and a new beginning for the parent.

Epilogue

In the healing of physical and sexual abuse, the end result is like many heroic epic stories-- a mysterious journey, sometimes delightful, more often frightening and courageous—to find oneself. Those who have truly healed from this kind of abuse have traveled the path of the unknown to rediscover their strength, fortitude and self-love in a new way. To deeply embrace one's authentic self is like remembering that "no matter where I go, here I am,"--presence, love and purpose are anchors for life. As one of my clients said in realizing the enormous healing she has been through from severe abuse, *"I'm the one I've been looking for. And I'm glad to finally know me."*

We are here to bring healing and fulfill our purposes that we agreed with Creator-of All in what we wanted to complete. And we can go beyond our expectation of what we thought we could accomplish. This is not a possibility but a reality. We have been given the gift to remember our connection to Creator-of-All by actually using ThetaHealing® to do just this.

It's an important daily exercise to give gratitude for our lives, for the many tools and gifts we have been given to heal, to move beyond the "healer heal thyself" paradigm, to know balance between caring for ourselves and sharing our gifts with others; and to realize that no matter where the journey of life takes us, we show up ready to embrace it with dignity, strength, courage and the child-like wonder and playfulness that is always within us.

Creator's Teachings:

◇ I know that Creator-of-All exists in the unknown.

◇ I know that wherever my life takes me, Creator-of-All is there.

◇ I know what it feels like and how to be more than my past wounds and abuse history.

◇ I know the possibility of accomplishing my soul purposes without the encumberment of my past traumas.

◇ I know what it feels like and how to surpass my expectation of being fulfilled in each level of my evolution with ease and grace.

◇ I know what it feels like and how to be fulfilled in just being who I am.

◇ I know what it feels like and how to recognize life as a precious gift.

◇ I know what it feels like and how to accept this precious gift of life.

◇ I know what it feels like and how to have gratitude for all that I've learned and released without regret.

> **"Life isn't about how to survive the storm...
> but how to dance in the rain."** *−Unknown*

Responsibility to Report Child Abuse by a Minister

> **"The time is always right to do the right thing."**
> *– Martin Luther King, Jr.*

Child Welfare Information Gateway is a service of the United States Department of Health and Human Services (DHHS). DHHS is the primary child protection agency of the federal government.[50] This site provides information about professionals in your state who are required by law to report abuse, how to report it, and to whom a report to. It also provides information about special rules related to ministerial confidentiality and a telephone number where one can call for advice on how to proceed.

Some persons must report. Every state has a statute which requires that reasonable suspicion or known instances of child abuse must be reported by certain persons to public authorities. Some states require that any person who reasonably suspects child abuse or has knowledge that a child has been abused is required to report it. For those persons who are required by law to report, their failure to report is a crime.

Anyone may report. In addition to those who must report child abuse, any person may report his suspicion or information to law enforcement authorities or state agencies which are charged with the duty to protect children.

Should ministers report? Should a minister report what s/he learns about child sex abuse, even if the information is confided in him? Under the statutes in some states, a minister may be legally compelled to report. If not legally compelled in the state where s/he serves, the minister may still conclude that he has a moral duty to report. Some statutes speak specifically to the duty of ministers to report. These reporting statutes may need to be understood in the light of other statutes which describe special rules about the testimony of a minister when it comes to the revelation of information he has gained in his ministerial capacity.

Should a minister feel conflicted about whether to report due to concerns about the clergy-penitent relationship, several pertinent factors come into consideration:

- In some states, clergy-penitent privilege is a professional code of conduct rather than a legal right granted under the appropriate law codes.
- If the minister learns of any abuse from another source other than the perpetrator of the crime, it is not a confession and is not covered under the privilege.
- If the perpetrator has told anyone else other than the minister about the abuse, the privilege has already been waived.
- If a minister has a moral objection in sharing information learned in a pastoral counseling session, that minister must weigh the legal and moral responsibility of protecting the child against the moral code of ethics of his position.

In general, if one remains uncertain as to what to do, the best thing is to call an attorney in your town, city, state, or country for clarification and/or talk to Creator about it.

Footnoted References

(1) Women and Men Against Sexual Harassments and other Abuses: http://www.tagnet.org/wash/abusedefstats.html

(2) Child Abuse Statistics: http://www.findcounseling.com/journal/child-abuse/child-abuse-statistics.html

(3) Abuse and Addiction: http://www.irvingstudios.com/child_abuse_survivor_monument/Addictions.htm

(4) Trauma, Post-Traumatic Stress Disorder and Secondary Trauma: http://www.womanabuseprevention.com/html/trauma__post-traumatic_stress_.html

(5 & 6) Wiping out bad memories: http://www.thenational.ae/article/20081030/FRONTIERS/68555036/1036/FOREIGN Pill to erase bad memories: Ethical furore over drugs 'that threaten human identity' http://www.dailymail.co.uk/news/article-1145777/Pill-erase-bad-memories-Ethical-furore-drugs-threaten-human-identity.htm

(7) Project MKULTRA: http://parascope.com/ds/mkultradocs.htm http://www.nytimes.com/packages/pdf/national/13inmate_ProjectMKULTRA.pdf

(8) Child Abuse Linked To Cancer In Adulthood: http://www.enotalone.com/article/19728.html
The Body Bears the Burden (on line): http://books.google.com/books?id=FosHgiUF5HkC&pg=PA74&lpg=PA74&dq=the+immune+suppression+diseases+can+be+linked+to+childhood+abuse%3F&source=bl&ots=sCe0JCRMk1&sig=-P_lBB6xl8RUz4J2IkX4nT4WFnw&hl=en&ei=4tJWSraHBYj8tAOm50y9Dg&sa=X&oi=book_result&ct=result&resnum=2 Suppression of cellular immunity in men with a past history of posttraumatic stress disorder: N. Kawamura; Y.Kim, N.Asukai Am J Psychiatry 2001 Mar;158(3):484-6

(9) Child Abuse & Neglect: Physical Abuse: http://emedicine.medscape.com/article/915664-overview

(10) Childhood trauma has life-long effect on genes and the brain: http://www.physorg.com/news154627743.html

(11) Cozolino, 2002

(12) Giarratano, 2004b

(13) Meaney, 2009

(14) *The British Journal of Psychiatry (2005)* 186: 121-125 Impact of childhood abuse on the clinical course of bipolar disorder: http://cat.inist.fr/?aModele=afficheN&cpsidt=16472849

(15) Child abuse can cause schizophrenia: http://www.eurekalert.org/pub_releases/2006-06/uom-mat061306.php

(16 & 17) Impact on the Physiology of the Brain: http://www.asca.org.au/displaycommon.cfm?an=1&subarticlenbr=194

(18) How to build a baby's brain: http://www.newsweek.com/id/95363/page/2

(19) Effects of Child Abuse on Adults: Childhood Abuse http://www.findcounseling.com/journal/child-abuse/survivors-childhood-abuse.html

(20) *Health Care for Women International,* 16:21-30): http://www.myalgia.com/abuse.htm

(21 & 22) Neural Systems Underlying the Suppression of Unwanted Memories: http://www.sciencemag.org/cgi/content/abstract/303/5655/232

(23) *Scientific American:* Where Are Old Memories Stored in the Brain? http://www.scientificamerican.com/article.cfm?id=the-memory-trace

(24) Hidden Feelings: http://www.associnpsychotherapy.com/HiddenFeelings.htm

(25) *Moving your Eyes Improves your Memory* by Melissa Wenner http://www.livescience.com/health/070425_eyes_memory.html

(26) *Repressed Memories* by Renee Frederickson, Ph.D., New York; Simon & Schuster, 1992. p. 92

(27) Sidran Institute glossary: http://www.sidran.org/sub.cfm? contentID=38&sectionid=4

(28) Heller and Heller (2001)

(29) *Repressed Memories* by Renee Frederickson, Ph.D. New York; Simon & Schuster, 1992. p. 94

(30) Descriptive Definition of Ritual Abuse: http://www.kalimu-nro.com/ritual_abuse.html

(31) *Family Violence & Sexual Assault Bulletin,* 9 (1993): A Critical Examination of the False Memory Syndrome, 21-; by Donald Barstow

(32) *False Memories, False Construct* by Julia Cutler Page, http://web.archive.org/web/20030608221633/http://www.femini-sta.com/v1n9/false-memory.html

FMS and its CIA connections: http://www.towardfreedom.com/home/content/view/67/69/

(33) *The Journal of Paedophilia* 3 (1993), Interview: Hollida Wakefield and Ralph Underwager, Paidika: 3; J. Geract. Profile of Pedophile: http://forbiddentopic.blogspot.com/2008/09/profile-of-pedophile.html

(34) Report on Behavior and Activities Reported by My Patients from 1988 to Present, Valerie Wolf, PhD, Presidential Advisory Commission hearings. 1998

(35) What is a Screen Memory? http://www.ra-info.org/faqs/ra_faq.shtml#screen

(36) How to you feel today? (pictures of feelings): http://www4.

informatik.uni-erlangen.de/~msrex/how-do-you-feel.html

(37) Child Sexual Abuse Is Serious and Wide-Spread. http://www. advocatesforyouth.org/index.php?option=com_content&task= view&id=410&Itemid=336

(38) Diagnosis: ADHD—or Is It Trauma? Hyperactive, yes. Attention problems, check. But it's not ADHD; by Maia Szalavitz for MSN Health & Fitness; Medically Reviewed By: George T. Grossberg, M.D. http://health.msn.com/health-topics/adhd/ articlepage.aspx?cp-documentid=100191637

(39) Betrayal Trauma: The Logic of Forgetting Childhood Abuse (1996) Jennifer J. Freyd, Ph.D.; Cambridge, MA: Harvard University Press. 1994 ISBN: 067406805; 0674068068 http://dynamic.uoregon.edu/~jjf/trauma.html

(40) Love and the Stockholm Syndrome by Dr Joseph M Carver, PhD http://counsellingresource.com/quizzes/stockholm/index.html

(41) Gunnar, 1998

(42) Louise Hayes' *Meditation on Inner Child:* http://www.esnips. com/doc/62090fa9-55ea-42e8-a785-1cf6b78ae373/Welcoming%20the%20Inner%20Child%20Meditation%20with%20 Louise%20Hay

(43) Dissociative Disorders-DID and DDNOS: http://ritualabuse. us/research/did/the-diagnosis-and-assessment-of-dissociative-identity-disorder/

http://journals.lww.com/jonmd/Abstract/1998/06000/Axis_ II_Pathology_in_Outpatients__with.5.aspx

(44) *Multiplicity: The New Science of Personality, Identity, and the Self* by Rita Carter. Copyright © 2008 http://www.msnbc. msn.com/id/24096581/

Intro to Archetype Work: http://www.jbactors.com/actingreading/archetypesacting.html

(45) *Multiple Journeys to One: Spiritual Stories of Integrating from Dissociative Identity Disorder* by Judy Dragon and Terry Popp; Dancing Serpents Press, 1999.

http://www.thetadnaactivation.com/judysbook/index.html [Note: Only used bookstores carry it as it is out of print.]

(46) Advanced ThetaHealing®: All-That-Is; Vianna Stibal; Rolling Thunder Publishing; 2009, pages 266-269

(47) *Healing the Shame that Binds You* by John Bradshaw; Health Communications, Inc, http://www.amazon.com/Healing-Shame-That-Binds-You/dp/0932194869

(48) *ThetaHealing*® by Vianna Stibal, Rolling Thunder Press, 2006. Page 163

(49) Leaving the family: http://ritualabuse.us/research/leaving-the-family-system-an-honorable-choice/

(50) Information Gateway of DHHS can be accessed at http://www.childwelfare.gov

Recommended Books

ThetaHealing®, Advance ThetaHealing®, Disease and Conditions by Vianna Stibal, Rolling Thunder Press. www.thetahealing.com

Facing Codependence; Pia Mellody, Harper San Francisco

Feelings Buried Alive Never Die; Karol K. Truman; Olympus Distributing; St. George, UT.; 2003

Homecoming: Reclaiming and Championing Your Inner Child, by John Bradshaw; Banton Books; 1993

Healing the Child Within by Charles Whitfield, M.D. Health Communications, Inc., 1989

Repressed Memories by Renee Frederickson, MD. Fireside/Parkside Recovery Book; Paperback - July 1, 1992. (book is readable online in sections), http://books.google.com/books?id=3HkXeL Y6IdIC&pg=PA182&lpg=PA182&dq=repressed+memories+by+ renee+frederickson&source=bl&ots=s1rECvdwBB&sig=2nWxDl crGeiQkoCS7kxLILeea3w&hl=en&ei=XedWSvDvD4PmsQPT04 30AQ&sa=X&oi=book_result&ct=result&resnum=1

The Body Remembers: The Psychophysiology of Trauma and Trauma Treatment by Babette Rothschild; Los Angeles, CA; www.trana.cin; 310-281-9646

The PTSD Workbook - Simple, Effective Techniques for Overcoming Traumatic Stress Symptoms by Mary Beth Williams and Soili Poijula. New Harbinger Publications, Inc. 5674 Shattuck Ave. Oakland, CA 94609, www.newharbinger.com ISBN 1-57224-282-5 This workbook gathers together "techniques and interventions used by PTSD experts around the world....Readers learn how to determine the type of trauma they experienced, identify their symptoms and learn...strategies to overcome them."

Betrayal Trauma by Jennifer Freyd Ph.D.; The logic of forgetting childhood abuse. Cambridge, MA: Harvard University Press. 1996 http://dynamic.uoregon.edu/~jjf/trauma.html

The Betrayal Bond: Breaking Free of Exploitive Relationships by Patrick J. Carnes HCI (November 01 1997)

Books about the effects and healing of Child Sexual Abuse on Men:
http://www.menweb.org/sexabuse.html
http://www.nomas.org/node/127

Books about the effects and healing of Child Sexual Abuse on Women:

Healing from the Trauma of Childhood Sexual Abuse: The Journey for Women; by Karen A. Duncan: http://search.barnesandnoble. com/Healing-from-the-Trauma-of-Childhood-Sexual-Abuse/ Karen-A-Duncan/e/9780275980849

Courage to Heal by Ellen Bass and Laura Davis: http://www.pow-ells.com/cgi-bin biblio?inkey=1-9780060950668-20

Secret Survivors by E. Sue Blume; ISBN-13:9780345419453; January 1998 http://browse.barnesandnoble.com/booksearch/re-sults.asp?ath=E.+Sue+Blume

Glossary

Abreaction– The discharge of energy [emotion] involved in recalling an event that has been repressed because it was consciously intolerable. The experience may be one of reliving the trauma as if it were happening in the present, complete with physical as well as emotional manifestations (also called revivification).

Amnesic barriers– Hidden separations between memories or alters.

Attachment disorder– Attachment is the process of bonding between an infant's or child's primary caretaker. Neglect and abuse can sever these bonds. Insecure attachments influence the developing brain which leads to a variety of symptoms-- difficulty with interactions with others (difficulty with genuine trust, intimacy, and affection); lack of self-esteem and self-control, learning disabilities, and optimum mental and physical health are affected. Symptoms of insecure attachment may be similar to common developmental and mental problems including ADHD, spectrum autism, depression, and anxiety disorders. http://helpguide.org/mental/parenting_bonding_reactive_attachment_disorder.htm

Body memories– When the stress of past traumatic memories of abuse take the form of physical problems that cannot be explained by the usual means (medical examinations, etc.). http://www.rainn.org/get-information/effects-of-sexual-assault/somatic-body-memories

Borderline Personality (or Borderline Schizophrenia)– Onset begins in early adulthood; low self-esteem; problems with impulsive, erratic behavior which can lead to troubled, unstable relationships in every area of life; fear of being left alone (abandoned) even if the threat of being abandoned is not real; rejection of others before others might even consider rejecting them– this fear may lead to frantic attempts to hold on to those around them and may cause them to become too dependent on others; temporary episodes of psychosis (paranoia and a loss of a sense of reality).

Child Sexual Abuse– The American Medical Association defines child sexual abuse as "the engagement of a child in sexual activities for which the child is developmentally unprepared and cannot give informed consented." Child sexual abuse is characterized by deception, force or coercion.

Depersonalization— A disconnection from one's body, environment and psyche as well as having difficulty relating to oneself in this reality; not really experiencing life but going through the motions (as being in a movie or dream).

Desensitization— Ways in which interaction or witnessing violence increases inappropriate detachment of feelings in response to a situation. Exposure to violent video games and the media increases aggressive thoughts, angry feelings, physiological arousal and aggressive behaviors, and decreases helpful behaviors. Hundreds of sound scientific studies demonstrate the social impact of brutalization by the media. http://www.sciencedaily.com/releases/2006/07/060727162108.htm, http://www.killology.com/art_trained_methods.htm

Dissociative Disorders– Trauma-based psychological disorders in which dissociation affects a person's functioning; disturbance, detachment or alteration in the normally integrative functions of thoughts, feelings, memory, action, identity, or awareness.

DID (Dissociative Identity Disorder)– Once known as Multiple Personality Disorder; a dissociative disorder; an ingenious way to survive repeated sadistic abuse and torture by dividing and compartmentalizing the personality to many. Experiences of flashbacks and intrusion of trauma memories, sometimes not until years after the childhood abuse, with dissociative experiences of distancing, "trancing out", feeling unreal, the ability to ignore pain, and feeling as if they were looking at the world through a fog.

DDNOS (Dissociative Disorder Not Otherwise Specified)— Similar to DID but does not meet all the criteria in the DSM-IV-TR

Dissociative Reaction— Symptoms of daydreaming, loose contact with reality and out-of-body experience to prevent being hurt, where the child reports watching an event from outside of the body.

DSM-IV-TR— The entire psychological category of Dissociative Disorders

Engram Banks- (see Free floating memories)

Flashbacks– A type of spontaneous abreaction common to victims of acute trauma. Also known as "intrusive recall," flashbacks have been categorized into four types:

• Dreams or nightmares
• Dreams from which the dreamer awakens but remains under the influence of the dream content and has difficulty making contact with reality
• Conscious flashbacks, in which the person may or may not lose contact with reality and which may be accompanied by multimodal hallucinations
• Unconscious flashbacks, in which a person "relives" a traumatic event with no awareness at the time or later of the connection between the flashback and the past trauma.
Putnam, *Diagnosis and Treatment of Multiple Personality Disorder,* pp. 236-237.

Flooding– The process of becoming overwhelmed by intrusive emotions, sensory experiences, or unconscious memories arising to the surface quickly.

Free floating memories– Programs from others that we accept when unconscious. Symptoms develop. The person replays the trauma in the conscious waking world. (Basic ThetaHealing®- p. 106)

Government abuse of children– Systematic use of children, often without parental consent, for purposes of mind, body, pathogenic and/or drug experimentation, mind control and other perverse abuse. http://www.geocities.com/area51/Shadowlands/6583/project121.html

Grounding– Reality-based awareness in the here and now; a sense of connectedness to one's self and environment.

Host personality– In dissociation, it can either be the original birth child, or it can be an alter that is the main personality presented to the outside world. Most alters protect the host personality from the memories of the trauma.

Inner Parent– Archetype of a loving, nurturing, safe, and supportive mother and/or father that can be created by the client in the inner world to replace an abusive parent.

Obsessive-compulsive disorder– An anxiety disorder characterized by recurrent, unwanted thoughts (obsessions) and/or repetitive behaviors (compulsions) such as hand washing, counting, checking, or cleaning, often performed with the hope of preventing obsessive thoughts or making them go away; performing these so-called "rituals," provides only temporary relief, but stopping them markedly increases anxiety.

Psychic Driving– Intent to break down the subject's personality so it can then be used with some efficacy in establishing a new personality; use of massive electric shock therapy, drugs and restraining the person for hours with auditory tapes looping with behavior deemed appropriate; Dr. Ewen Cameron of McGill University in Canada was responsible for such horrific abuse.

Traumatic hypervigilance– The experience of being constantly tense and "on guard" which is a symptom of PTSD. There is an increased awareness and scanning of the surrounding environment to identify potential sources of danger often accompanied by changes in behavior including paranoia.

Victim Trust—Due to poor discernment, those who have been abused are often unable to pick up the cues for who is worthy to trust and either trusts everyone or no one.

Index

A

aberrant behaviors, 11

abortions, 52

abreaction, 29, 99

acting out memories, 21

addictions, 84-85

ADHD, 33

adrenaline, 10, 33, 47

alien abduction, 26

alien experimentation, 8 (exploratory, rape, egg harvesting, hybriding, DNA changes)

amnesic barriers, 17

amygdala, 10, 99

ancestral lineages, 70

anger, 35, 66, 71, 72, 82

anxiety dreams, 19

armoring, 32

attachment disorder, 47, 99

authentic self, 53

avoidance, 3

B

backlash, 24

betrayal of trust, 46-47

betrayal trauma, 46

bi-polar, 10

Black Witchcraft, 8

blessings, 72

body's intelligence, 28

bonded to perpetrator, 50

bonding, 45, 50, 51

borderline schizophrenia, 10, 99

boundaries, 40-46, 86

brain chemistry, 47

breathing exercise, 71

C

cellular trauma, 68

Child Welfare Information Gateway, 90

childhood abuse, 4, 100

CIA, 24

circumcision, 8

clergy-penitent privilege, 91

cloning, 8

co-consciousness, 60

co-dependency, 41

cognizant state, 17

collage, 28

complete integration, 61

confrontation, 74

contained sacred space, 71

Continuum of Dissociation, 59-61

coping mechanisms, 53

corpus callosum, 10

corroborating data, 74

cortex activity, 10

cortisol, 10

covert technologies, 25

crystal layout, 28

D

degrees of dissociation, 60

depersonalization, 100

desensitization, 12, 100

depression, 10, 11, 47

dialoguing, 35

Dissociative Disorder Not Otherwise Specified (DDNOS), 47.
59, 101

dissociated feelings, 16

dissociative disorders, 10, 100

Dissociative Identity Disorder DID,
47, 59, 62, 68, 100

dissociative reaction, 32, 101

digging process, 37

digital penetration, 8

DNA, 9

Dr. Bessel van der Kolk, 24

dreams, 19

DSM-IV-TR, 24, 101

E

emotional incest, 14

emotions, 30

empowerment, 69, 84

engram banks, 69

entities, 67, 69

epigenetic marks, 9

extracting beliefs, 36

F

False Memory Syndrome
Foundation FMSF, 24

family rules, 74

family structures, 73

fashbacks, 19, 101

flooding, 22

forgiveness, 81-85

frontal cortex, 15

frontal lobe functioning, 10

fusion, 61

G

gene expression, 9

generational curse, 79

glucocorticoid (cortisol), 9

government experimentation, 8,
102

grand dissociation, 59

grounding, 102

H

Heart Song exercise, 80

hippocampus, 10, 12

host (core) personality, 60, 102

hypervigilance, 103

hypnosis, 24-26

I

implants, 18

inappropriate touching, 8

Inner Child, 28, 53-59, 70

Inner Parent, 47, 102

integration, 56

internalize, 13

J

journal writing, 28

L

limbic system, 10, 16

M

Manchurian candidates/
  assassination, 8

Meet your Inner Child
  meditation, 55-59

memories, 11, 27, 57, 71

  accordion memories, 22, 23

  acting-out memories, 21

  bizarre memories, 23

  body memories, 20, 99

  forgotten memory, 29

  free floating memories, 68, 69,
  102

  image memories, 19

  implanted memories, 23, 25

  memory erasing, 4

  memory imprints, 68

memory retrieval, 69

  recalling/recalled (conscious)
  memories, 15, 16, 18

  repressed feeling memories,
  22, 29

  repressed memories, 16, 17, 27,
  82

  screen memories, 25, 26

  somatic memories, 20

  spliced memories, 11

  spontaneous memories, 18

  unwanted memories, 15

  Verifying Emerging or
  Recovered Memories, 73

  verify memories, 73, 74

mind control, 4

mind control programming, 8

ministerial confidentiality, 90

multiple personalities, 59

N

Near-Death Experience, 47

neglect, 8

neural connections, 10

neuro-endocrine alterations, 10

nightmares, 19, 62

non-dominant handwriting, 28

O

Obsessive Compulsive Disorder
  OCD, 10, 102

P

pastoral counseling session, 91

patterns of abuse, 11

patterns of trauma, 76

patterns of unveiling, 18

pedophiles, 24

perpetrators, 24

physical abuse, 7, 47

physical symptoms of abuse:

chills, 21

constipation, cramping, 20

diarrhea, 20

eating disorders, 11

endometriosis, 21

frigidity, 21

gastrointestinal distress, 12

headaches, 20

irregular menses, 20

migraines, 20

muscle spasms, 21

musculoskeletal complaints, 12

painful intercourse, 21

palpitations, 20

respiratory ailments, 12

sexual dysfunction, 12

sleep disorders, 11

stiff neck, 20

sweating, 21

tinnitus, 20

TMJ issues, 21

tremors, 21

visual disturbances, 20

pornographic material, 8

positive ego strengthening, 74

promiscuity, 12, 41

prostitution (child sex slavery),8

protection, 32

psychic driving, 8, 102

psychogenic amnesia, 24

psychological abuse, 8

psychologists, 24

Post Traumatic Stress Disorder
PTSD, 10, 29, 47, 62, 68

R

receptors, 9

receptor sites, 29

release cords, 86

reliving the abuse, 29

repression, 15

Rescue the Inner Child, 70

retrieval, 24

ritual abuse, 8, 47

S

safe place, 70

safety, 69

Satanism, 8, 26

schizophrenia, 10

Secondary Post Traumatic
Syndrome, 4

self hatred, 81

self respect, 81

self-acceptance, 81

self-cut, 32

self-love, 81

sensorimotor processes, 24

sexual abuse, 8, 47

    verbal sexual abuse, 8

somatic responses, 20

soul fragment, 13

Stockholm Syndrome, 51

suppression, 15

T

teleportation, 8

torture, 8

toxic shame, 73

trauma bonding, 51

trauma energy, 20

trauma, 12, 26

traumatic amnesia, 24

truth verifying, 74

U

unconscious, 29

United States Department of
    Health and Human Services
    (DHHS), 90

V

vaginal/genital mutilation, 8

victim trust, 103

virtual reality, 8, 25, 26

W

waywards, 61, 69

wonder child, 53